So Long, Normal

Living and Loving the Free Fall of Faith

STUDY GUIDE | FIVE SESSIONS

Laura Story

with Beth Graybill

HarperChristian Resources

So Long, Normal Study Guide

Requests for information should be addressed to:

HarperChristian Resources, 3900 Sparks Dr. SE, Grand Rapids, Michigan 49546

ISBN 978-0-310-14231-7 (softcover)
ISBN 978-0-310-14232-4 (ebook)

HarperChristian Resources titles may be purchased in bulk for church, business, fundraising, or ministry use. For information, please e-mail ResourceSpecialist@ChurchSource.com.

First Printing June 2021 / Printed in the United States of America

Contents

Of Note

The quotations interspersed throughout this study guide and the between-sessions materials are from the book, *So Long, Normal* and the video curriculum *So Long, Normal* by Laura Story. All other resources including the small-group questions and session introductions have been written by Beth Graybill in collaboration with Laura Story.

Welcome

READY FOR ADVENTURE

Have you ever found yourself paralyzed by fear in the inevitable changes of life? Me too. In those moments, we're tempted to lean on any sense of normalcy, predictability, security, and control. But God often calls us to something better, beyond our range of fear.

While we may hear God's voice, following God's lead is another story. There are obstacles in our way: attachment to comfort, a desire for everything to remain the same, and anything else we grip tightly with two hands when our circumstances change.

Change is inevitable, but there is still a way to thrive: saying so long to normal. When we say goodbye to normal, our joy and peace are no longer tethered to the predictability of our circumstances. And it's in this place we can truly experience the abundant life God has to offer his children.

> **"He has made everything beautiful in its time. Also, he has put eternity into man's heart, yet so that he cannot find out what God has done from the beginning to the end."**
>
> **Ecclesiastes 3:11 ESV**

This five-session study helps us recognize our attachments to the many "normal" things in our daily lives that keep us from experiencing the kind of life God intends—the kind of life God defines in Scripture. The good news is we're not alone.

So many characters in the Bible had attachments that kept them from living the life God intended for them. They had to choose between something they could hold on to with tangible, physical assurance, *or* release those things in order to embrace the abundant life God promised.

It all came down to whether or not these characters were willing to let go of *normal* and step into the excitement of life with God. And the adventure, for them and for us, begins with the first step of trust.

This study is my invitation to you to go on this adventure together.

Laura

SESSION

1

What's So Bad about Normal?

GROUP STUDY

INTRODUCTION

Leader, read this section aloud to the group:

Have you ever tried to grab your breath on a cold morning? It may seem like an odd question, but it's undoubtedly something we've all tried to do at some point in our lives. Catching our breath is like trying to maintain a sense of "normal." And at some point along the way, I realized the normal life I sought was like a vapor. Whenever it appeared within reach, I was unable to grasp it.

Normal. It's a fairly subjective word, yet we all seem to understand what it means. Normal is often defined as "conforming to a standard; usual, typical or expected." And it seems to be the gravity we seek with an innate desire to have our feet planted on something solid rather than having our lives suspended in mid-air. Normal appears to offer the steady we want, the comfort we need, and the accountability required to keep us on task.

As anyone who knows me can attest, my life has been anything but dictionary-definition normal. My idea of normal came crashing down when my husband was diagnosed with a brain tumor during the second year of our marriage. After his diagnosis, a complicated surgery, concerning days in the ICU, and a long recovery at home, Martin still lives with short-term memory loss and a substantial vision deficit. His inability to see well or remember the smallest details make our life as a family anything but normal.

My story may look different than yours, but each of us has something in our lives that has forced us to let go of whatever normalcy we envisioned. And I've lived long enough to know no one's life has turned out exactly the way they had planned. Every one of us has endured uninvited change. Every one of us will again be forced to wave goodbye to normal.

But there is something deeply comforting about the normal ordinariness of life that draws us to this ideal. We all long for security, for stability, and firm footing. In fact, we crave it. Have you ever wondered why we crave it? I believe it's because we were designed by an orderly God to thrive in an orderly world. But then sin happened, and the steady path beneath the feet of humanity shifted and became shaky. Ever since, our normal has been distorted. Just like Adam and Eve, we have no choice but to say so long to a normal life and step out beyond the garden of our lives until Jesus returns and the garden is restored.

Believe this: whenever our life shifts and shakes, it's ultimately for our benefit that good things are shaken from our grip, even when it feels like a loss. My hope for you and me is that whenever we face the loss of normal, we encounter God. And not in a way that puts a spiritual Band-Aid on the grief we're experiencing, but in a way that helps us recognize God is working in and through our circumstances beyond our imagining.

When God is our foundation, we can learn to say so long to normal and all the good things God lovingly shakes from our lives. But first, we have to acknowledge our desire for normal and how it affects our everyday lives. Let's do the hard, courageous work together.

God is our sure and steady hope who guides us to embrace the beautiful story unfolding before our very eyes as we say so long to normal.

TALK ABOUT IT

Take 10–15 minutes to respond to the opening message from Laura. Then take turns answering the following questions in preparation for the video teaching. Use this section each week to get your hearts and minds focused and ready for Laura's teaching.

- Share about a time in your childhood, teenage years, or adult life when you felt less than normal. As you look back, what factors contributed to this feeling for you?

—or—

- What does "normal" mean to you?

> *Rather than defining normal, it may be easier to recognize the absence of it.*

WATCH VIDEO SESSION ONE (17 MINUTES)

Use the video streaming access code on the inside of the front cover of your study guide or use the DVD to watch this session.

• VIDEO TEACHING NOTES

As you watch the video teaching for this session, use the following outline to record anything that stands out to you.

A departure from normal

What is normal anyway?

What would it take to feel normal?

Leaving normal for adventure with God

Saying goodbye to normal requires a heart change

Finding freedom, peace, and joy

Hebrews: the book of "better things"

Shaken (Hebrews 12:28 and Haggai 2:6–8)

God as the source of our shaking

The faulty foundation of our lives

God's calling to us

Saying so long to normal

Having courage isn't about the absence of fear. It's acknowledging that fear and being willing to take that next step anyway.

GROUP DISCUSSION

Read each question and take time for group members to give honest and thoughtful responses.

1. What comes to your mind when you hear Laura talk about this idea of being normal? What are some of the negative connotations and positive meanings of the word *normal*?

2. Where does the pressure to feel or be normal come from for you? Is it an internal idea or an external pressure? Briefly explain.

> *It doesn't matter if normal is something you never knew, something you've always tried to attain, or something you've grown tired of, you're invited on a thrilling journey to leave normal because what God has in store is better.*

Select volunteers to read the following passages aloud to the group and discuss the questions with each:

Hebrews 12:25–29 ESV

3. What are some of the "good" or "normal" things that consume your focus and crowd out God's invitation to you to live with a kingdom mentality? What could you do to refocus your attention and your priorities?

4. What does it mean for us to receive an unshakeable kingdom? How have you sensed God shaking up your life?

Our loving God not only allows the shaking in our lives, but he is at times the source and the cause of our shaking.

Select a group member to read this passage out loud:

Haggai 2:6–10 NIV

5. In whatever shaking you are experiencing right now, what emotions rise to the surface? Are there any positive results of this shaking?

6. Tell about some of the ways you've watched God shake things up for someone close to you. How did things turn out for that person or group of people? What did you learn by watching the situation?

God shakes the less sturdy things out of our lives out of his kindness and mercy.

Select a group member to read this passage out loud:

Ephesians 3:20–21 NIV

7. Laura shared her zipline story and the courage it took to let go and trust God. Where do you need to let go and trust God? What is one area of your life where you need to surrender your longing for normal or let go of your tight grip for control?

8. What is the "immeasurably more" you are asking God for right now? In what situation do you need God to give you faith to believe he can do something good?

God promises to do more through us than we could ask or imagine.

Memory Verse

Commit to memorizing one verse or passage each week as a group, as you practice saying so long to normal. This week's verses are:

> "Therefore let us be grateful for receiving a kingdom that cannot be shaken, and thus let us offer to God acceptable worship, with reverence and awe, for our God is a consuming fire."
>
> **Hebrews 12:28–29 ESV**

CLOSING PRAYER

Spend time in your group praying in some of the following directions:

- Pray for your group members as they seek to understand the longing they have for normal or the sense of security they get from normal in their lives.

- Ask the Holy Spirit to show you areas in your life where you need to let go of normal and say yes to God.
- Thank God for how he shakes things up in us to loosen our grip on the things we hold tightly in order that he can do more with our lives.
- Celebrate the fact that God exceeds our expectations and our imagination for the courageous and adventurous life he calls us to live.

Record prayer requests here for easy reference to pray for one another throughout the week:

SESSION

1

What's So Bad about Normal?

BETWEEN-SESSIONS PERSONAL BIBLE STUDY

Before your next group meeting, spend time with the following Bible study lessons. There are five lessons. Do as much as you have time for but make it a priority to engage the Scripture a few minutes each day.

• LESSON ONE: BACK TO THE GARDEN

For most of us, there is something within that likes to create patterns and stick to them, even for the most free-spirited people. But we must recognize that our desire to create normal life patterns isn't something new. It dates back to the Garden. And we don't just like to create these patterns; we actually *crave* them. We all long for the security, stability, and sure footing that our patterns (even patterns of chaos) bring to our lives.

But have you ever stopped to think about how this yearning found its way into the fabric of who we are as humans? And what is it about normal patterns that feel so safe and comforting? Orderliness is the universal experience of all humans—it shows up in our rituals, rhythms, and routines. It shows up in our individual and collective expressions of "normal."

Answer the following questions as you consider life's rituals and routines:

- **Read Ecclesiastes 3** and consider what Solomon, the author, means when he writes about the "set[ting] of eternity in the heart" (verse 11 NIV). How do we experience this God-given gift and burden of experiencing eternity in our hearts?

- Why or how does it soothe us to know that there is an appointed time for every event, even death, this side of heaven?

- What rituals do you stick to in your life? Do you have a morning ritual, a work ritual, and an evening ritual? What is it and why is it so important to you?

- **Read Genesis 1** and consider what it means to be made in the image of God and to reflect the cosmic order God created. How does our desire for normalcy reflect God's pattern of design for our world?

- **Read Genesis 2.** Pray for the courage and discipline to see your desire for normal, healthy patterns—such as the ones we see in the Creation story—as one of God's greatest gifts to the human experience.

"You have made us for yourself, and our hearts are restless until we can find peace in you."
Saint Augustine (354–430 AD)

• LESSON TWO: EAST OF EDEN

Isn't it fascinating to consider how everything in creation and our own lives was turned upside down because of Adam and Eve's sin? And yet, despite the disappointment of their fall from grace, we see the kindness and faithfulness of God. Where the serpent's question, "Indeed, has God said?" resulted in destruction, God's question, "Where are you?" resulted in restoration. As God lovingly pursued Adam and Eve, he walked them through a very deliberate process of confession, forgiveness, and reconciliation. On a whole other level, he "set eternity in their hearts" by offering them a promise of future deliverance.

This is the very same promise God offers to us today, and it's a promise to one day return things to a God-designed normal. But until then, our lives will be rocked and shaken in a world that lies "east of Eden." Until Jesus returns and the garden is restored, we will crave normal with a deep, intense heartache. And we will try to craft and create normal out of the broken pieces of our lives. It's important to acknowledge our desire for normal, and equally as important to acknowledge how this desire affects the choices we make in our everyday lives and in our world.

Adam and Eve were living life to its fullest until they ate the forbidden fruit and had to leave the garden. And I think we tend to do the same. We start to doubt God's promise. But living east of Eden reminds us of our dependence on the deliverance of Jesus. And while we wait upon his ultimate deliverance someday, he offers us little moments of deliverance in the here and now, east of Eden.

Begin with prayer. Ask God to show you how you've deflected his promises for your life, and how you've been living "east of Eden" by choice. Seeking happiness outside of his will looks like choosing to do life on your own, depending on others to fulfill your desires instead of God, or doubting

God's faithfulness to follow through on his promises to you. If you like writing out your prayers, use the space provided below:

Reflect on God's Word. Take time to read Genesis 3, and then read Psalm 139:23–24 NIV. Make this psalm your prayer for a few quiet moments.

> **"Search me, God, and know my heart;**
> **Test me and know my anxious thoughts.**
> **See if there is any offensive way in me,**
> **And lead me in the way everlasting."**

After a few moments of prayer, write down two or three specific areas of your life where you feel, or have felt in the past, like God was holding out on you. For each area, answer these questions:

- How have you taken matters into your own hands in this particular area of your life?
- What happened as a result?
- How has God shown you his faithfulness and his love despite your refusal to accept or follow his ways?
- How will you let go and trust God's plans for your life?

Think about specific instances and actions. Ponder the actions or patterns God is asking you to give up so he can fulfill his promise to you.

AREA ONE:

AREA TWO:

AREA THREE:

Identify one specific action step you will take today or this week to live a life more surrendered to his will and his ways.

MY ACTION GOAL:

> *God placed man in the garden of Eden to cultivate and keep it, to give him meaningful and purposeful work. Together, Adam and Eve worked in the garden, and their labor was not toilsome . . . they didn't resent its place in their lives. It was simply the natural rhythm of life that had been ordained by God the Father.*

• *LESSON THREE: TRUST*

Let's be honest. All of us are prone to placing too much trust in our own abilities at times. For some of us, it's our planning and our abilities to get things done. For others, it's our ability to engage others who will plan and get things done for us. Either way, we feel pretty confident in our decision making and our skills. When we focus our attention on ourselves and what we have control over in our lives, we lose sight of the ultimate purpose of our lives: to trust God. We kick into autopilot when our lives are filled with ease and relatively free of hardships. And we begin to live our lives seeking less and less consultation with God.

It's during these times that we find ourselves most susceptible to the consequences of placing our trust in ourselves, rather than in God. It's when we are most susceptible to the whispered question of the serpent—"Indeed, has God said?"—that leads us to doubt what we're called or not called to do. For many of us, it's when we have no hurdles or resistance and we're living on autopilot that we settle into normal. But we've forgotten a gap exists between God's version of normal and our version. Saying goodbye to our version of normal means saying goodbye to the misguided ways we trust ourselves as we transfer that trust back to God.

Answer the following questions as you consider trusting God:

- **Read Numbers 20:1–12** and consider what happened to Moses and the Israelites when they refused to trust God. We know that things ultimately worked out for their good (Joshua 1), and yet their misguided trust caused a massive delay in their redemption story. How has your own misguided trust caused a delay in your life? To where or to what was God leading you when you chose to derail the journey by trusting yourself, or others, more than trusting God? How has God redeemed you and your story despite your delay?

- **Read Psalm 62.** What reasons does the author give for trusting God? In what way have you known these reasons to be true for you in your experience of God?

- **Read Proverbs 3:5–6.** According to this passage, what does it look like to trust in God? How are you trusting God in this way? Rewrite these verses as a personal prayer:

— *I will trust in the Lord with all my heart* (list your emotions),

— *Lean not on my own understanding* (list your thoughts),

— *And in all my ways acknowledge him* (how will you do this today?),

— *And he will make my paths straight* (write your prayer, i.e., "Father

— give me the faith to trust you with my plans and with my life.")

Until Jesus returns and the garden is restored, we'll continue to crave a sense of order and normalcy that will always be beyond our reach.

• LESSON FOUR: UNSHAKEABLE CHANGE

Change comes in many shapes and through many different circumstances. Every one of us has experienced something in life that has shaken us into change. We've experienced job loss, a health diagnosis, the death of a loved one, the high school graduation of a child, or a geographic change due to marriage, school, or job relocation. Change can be a wild card, introducing an element of uncertainty in our lives and most likely causing stress. We can try to avoid it, but to live is to change.

And we know change often means that upheaval follows—some kind of sturdiness and stability give way. Change shakes up our lives and reflects what we've learned long ago in the Creation story of the garden: normal is no longer normal; it's distorted. So when change shakes up the normal in our lives, how do we become the kind of people who see that the "normal" being shaken up by change is most often our distorted view of normal, anyway?

According to the Bible, our lives can get shaky and our sense of normal can disappear, but we do not have to be shaken by this change. The Bible clearly speaks about a type of shaking that our loving God allows. And this kind of shaking isn't random or unsupervised; it's actually purposeful with benefits for our lives. The shaking God allows in our lives is a means to an end. God is leveraging our circumstances to be sturdier and more stable, and to remind us we have an unshakeable faith in him.

Reflect on these reminders of God's promises to work all things out for our good:

> **"'Once more I will shake not only the earth but also the heavens' . . . so that what cannot be shaken may remain."**
>
> **Hebrews 12:26–27 NIV**

> **"And we know that in all things God works for the good of those who love him, who have been called according to his purpose."**
>
> **Romans 8:28 NIV**

> **"So then, those who suffer according to God's will should commit themselves to their faithful Creator and continue to do good."**
>
> **1 Peter 4:19 NIV**

How has God allowed change to shake things up in your life according to his purpose? In what specific ways has this contributed to an unshakeable faith in you?

Part of our journey of saying so long to normal is when we can learn to say so long to all of those things God lovingly shakes from our life.

• LESSON FIVE: A FIRM FOUNDATION

On a spiritual level, God in his mercy may allow our lives to be shaken for the sole purpose of exposing a faulty foundation. It's in God's *kindness* that he allows us to keep from building our lives on a faulty foundation that will eventually give away. It's in God's *love* that he allows us to experience trials so we learn to let go of the false building blocks of this world, and in doing so, understand the importance of clinging to only those things that cannot be shaken. God allows the changing and the shaking to occur in our lives so we can say goodbye to our distorted view of normal and find our way back to a firm foundation in him.

A peaceful (or courageous) life requires a firm foundation. When we allow God to be the source of our firm foundation, we stop looking to all of the good things we have holding up the foundation of our lives: our relationships, our accomplishments, our service, our knowledge, and we start looking to God. When we see God as our source, then everything else becomes a blessing in our lives and not a necessity to our foundation. When God is our foundation, we can let everyone and everything else off the hook.

Read these words of Jesus as he talks about himself as our foundation:

> **"Therefore everyone who hears these words of mine and puts them into practice is like a wise man who built his house on the rock. The rain came down, the streams rose, and the winds blew and beat against that house; yet it did not fall, because it had its foundation on the rock. But everyone who hears these words of mine**

> **and does not put them into practice is like a foolish man who built his house on sand. The rain came down, the streams rose, and the winds blew and beat against that house, and it fell with a great crash."**
>
> **Matthew 7:24–27 NIV**

Now journal your answers to these questions:

- As we consider what makes up our foundation, take a moment to think about what things in life bring you joy and make you feel valued. Success? Your schedule? Now consider how you would handle it if those things were taken away.

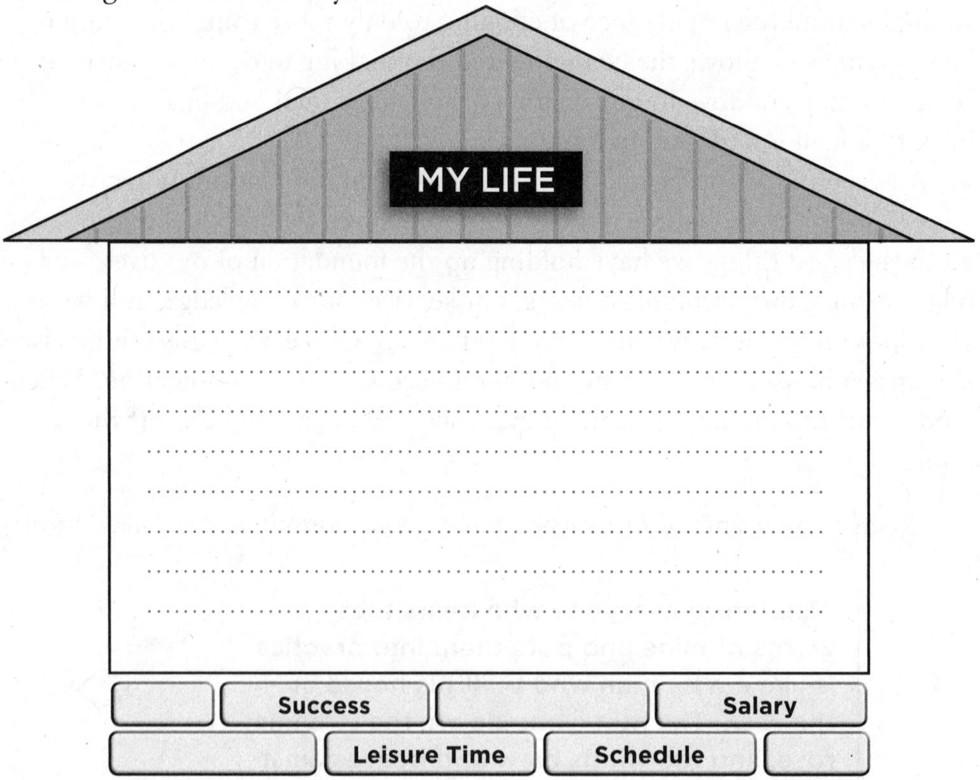

- Who or what do you need to let off the hook? Meaning, are there important people or pieces of your foundation that may belong in your life but don't belong as part of your foundation?

- Now that you can see these things as faulty foundations, how does this change your perception of God allowing these things to give way? Can you see how God's removal of that faulty foundation was an act of kindness rather than a malicious one?

Pray for courage to embrace change and allow God to shake things from your life so you're left with him as your firm foundation. Doing this will prepare you to say goodbye to normal so you can say yes to God's adventure for your life.

> *God cares too much to leave us standing on shifting sand when he rescued us from the dominion of darkness to stand on the only sure foundation: himself.*

RECOMMENDED READING

As you reflect on what God is teaching you through this session, you may want to read chapters 1 and 2 of *So Long, Normal* by Laura Story. And consider reading chapter 3 as you get ready for the next session.

SESSION

2

So Long, Familiar

GROUP STUDY

INTRODUCTION

Leader, read this section aloud to the group:

As I've sung more times than I can remember, the blessings God gives us aren't always the ones we anticipate, like the time Martin and I were homeless for three months. Just because we answer God's nudge to move out from our comfort zone—our familiar town, the community in which we raised our kids, whatever our idea of "home" is—doesn't mean the journey will be easy, even when it's a journey of faith.

Although the Israelites left Egypt with hearts full of faith, gleefully expectant of what God would do for them, this sentiment of faith and anticipation of a better life was short-lived. Rather than evaluating their wilderness predicament based on what they always held to be true about God, they changed their view based on their circumstances. They failed to see God for who he was. Ultimately, they failed to see God as faithful. My sadness for Israel is genuine because I too can forget that God is faithful to his promises.

Have you ever been tempted to respond this same way? Your bills are piling up, so you question whether God is really faithful as your Provider. You're chastised or picked on for your faith at work or school, and you wonder whether God is faithful as your Defender. You feel alone in this world, and you wonder whether God is faithful as the one who promised to never leave you or forsake you. To be human is to doubt and grasp for what's familiar.

Look at your own life today. Consider the normal patterns that provide a sense of stability for you and your family. These aren't bad things at all. In fact, a routine life allows us to avoid the chaos that always seems to be knocking at our doors. And yet, if normal is our goal, our highest value, we may very well miss the extraordinary work God has in store. Just like Israel, we may be choosing the bondage of normal over the promise of better things.

The Israelites couldn't dream big enough to imagine what God was about to do. And what if the same is true for us too? As hard as it is to believe, freedom and deliverance beyond our wildest dreams often await us if we only trust God, if we are willing to embrace faith and say so long to the familiar.

> *In all of our Moses moments, may we be reminded God is right there with us, and may we come to a place of saying so long, home, and find our dwelling place in God alone.*

MEMORY VERSE FROM LAST SESSION

Memorizing Scripture is a helpful habit as you learn to say so long to normal. Repeat last week's memory verses out loud as a group.

> **"Therefore let us be grateful for receiving a kingdom that cannot be shaken, and thus let us offer to God acceptable worship, with reverence and awe, for our God is a consuming fire."**
>
> **Hebrews 12:28–29 ESV**

TALK ABOUT IT

Take 10–15 minutes to respond to the opening message from Laura. Then take turns answering the following questions in preparation for the video teaching. Use this section each week to get your hearts and minds focused and ready for Laura's teaching.

- Tell about a time when your faith became your own, not the faith of your parents or your church community. As you look back, what factors contributed to this discovery for you?

—or—

- What does "faith" mean to you?

> *More often than not, God simply calls us out from the familiar and into faith.*

WATCH VIDEO SESSION TWO (19 MINUTES)

Use the video streaming access code on the inside of the front cover of your study guide or use the DVD to watch this session.

• VIDEO TEACHING NOTES

As you watch the video teaching for this session, use the following outline to record anything that stands out to you.

What is your steady?

Embracing faith rather than the familiar

Studying the Bible

Apart from Jesus, there are no perfect people in the Bible.

Three Bible characters called to leave behind normal:

— Mary, the mother of Jesus (Luke 1:30–31, 38)

— Ruth (Ruth 1:1, 15–17)

— Hagar (Genesis 16:7–13)

Living out our faith

The God that gave us such a great faith didn't do so that we would cling to the familiar normal for security.

Crucial questions:

— Have I held too tightly to my own best-made plan? Or, like Mary, have I submitted to God's plan?

— Have I sought security in the easy and the familiar? Or, like Ruth, have I followed God into an epic story, too great for me to have even dreamed?

— Have I resigned myself to being overlooked and deserted, allowing the choices of others to define me? Or, like Hagar, am I listening to the voice of "El Roi," the God who sees me?

When our plans fail us, and our family and friends leave us, and our future looks bleak, may we find God to be the rock on which we stand. The foundation of our faith

> "Truly he is my rock and my salvation;
> he is my fortress, I will not be shaken."
>
> **Psalm 62:6 NIV**

• GROUP DISCUSSION

Read each question and take time for group members to give honest and thoughtful responses. You will revisit the questions Laura asked at the end of this session in your personal study time.

1. How would you answer Laura's first question: *What is your steady, meaning, what keeps you sane?*

2. According to Laura's teaching, what does faith have to do with saying goodbye to normal?

Simply put, saying so long to normal means embracing faith rather than the familiar.

Select volunteers to read the following passages aloud to the group and discuss the questions with each:

Luke 1:26–45 NIV

3. How did Mary choose faith rather than the familiar?

4. Like Mary, how have you had to set aside your plan to embrace God's plan for your life?

God is the real hero of the Bible. Let's keep in mind how these stories fit into the greater story of God working out his purposes for his glory and for our good.

Select a group member to read this passage out loud:

Ruth 1:1–18 ESV

5. How did Ruth choose faith rather than the familiar? And what does Ruth's situation tell us about her faith in Naomi's God?

6. Like Ruth, how have you embraced a new life of trusting God alone for your provision? What were the circumstances that led you to trust God for your needs?

Life as a widow in even the best of biblical times meant a life of reliance on someone else for provision. But that's what makes Ruth such a remarkable woman.

Select a group member to read this passage out loud:

Genesis 16 ESV

7. How did Hagar choose faith rather than the familiar even after she ran from her pain?

8. Like Hagar, how have you run from pain? And how has God been the "God who sees you" by protecting you in the midst of your pain and transforming your faith?

God often engages his people with questions for their benefit, to draw out the truth that he already knows but that we need to say out loud.

Memory Verse:

Commit this verse to memory this week:

> "Truly he is my rock and my salvation; he is my fortress, I will not be shaken."
>
> **Psalm 62:3 NIV**

CLOSING PRAYER

Spend time in your group praying in some of the following directions:

- Pray for your group members as they seek to let go of their best-made plans and follow God's leading in their lives.
- Ask the Holy Spirit to help you embrace your faith and step out of the familiar as you pursue his best for your life.
- Thank God for how he loves you and protects you.
- Celebrate the fact that God sees you even when you feel overlooked, deserted, or left behind by others, just like he saw Mary, Ruth, and Hagar.

Record prayer requests here for easy reference to pray for one another throughout the week:

SESSION

2

So Long, Familiar

BETWEEN-SESSIONS

PERSONAL BIBLE STUDY

Before your next group meeting, spend time with the following five Bible study lessons. Do as much as you have time for, but make it a priority to engage the Scripture a few minutes each day.

• LESSON ONE: THE JOURNEY AHEAD

Read Exodus 14 and 15. Surveying the book of Exodus is a bit of a roller coaster ride. It sounds like the drama reminiscent of a lovestruck middle-school girl, or maybe even past seasons of our lives. It reminds me of the time my husband and I were in between jobs and homeless for three months (more on that in chapter 3 of the book). But I'm often thankful God tells us a story about people more like me and you, rather than a story about people who are always confident, agreeable, and grateful. God tells a story about people who are longing to know what lies on the journey ahead. And if we're honest with ourselves, we are those people too.

I don't know about you, but I follow God much better when he gives me a map beforehand to let me know where I'm going. And there are times when I'd like to go in a different direction than where he's taking me. The truth is, I want to go wherever God asks me to go, but sometimes my desire for comfort and familiarity gets the best of me. But what if we stopped questioning and doubting God, and started following and trusting him with every turn of our lives? We would be like the Israelites after they crossed the Red Sea, grateful to God, rather than the Israelites who, moments later, forgot God's rescue and doubted their survival in the desert, grumbling to Moses about God.

When we trust God with the journey that lies ahead, no matter the twists and turns of our lives, we trade our grumbling for gratitude. Let's remember the stories of Moses, Mary, Ruth, and Hagar in light of their journeys with God.

Revisit the story of Moses from today's Scripture reading and the questions Laura asked at the end of her video teaching for session two:

- Have I forged my own way when faced with decisive moments? Or, like Moses, have I been willing to let God lead me?

- Have I held too tightly to my own best-made plan? Or, like Mary, have I submitted to God's plan?

- Have I sought security in the easy and the familiar? Or, like Ruth, have I followed God into an epic story, too great for me to have even dreamed?

- Have I resigned myself to being overlooked and deserted, allowing the choices of others to define me? Or, like Hagar, am I listening to the voice of "El Roi," the God who sees me?

God's consistency and care should give us confidence whenever we find ourselves feeling abandoned, forgotten, or homeless. Or uncertain of the journey ahead.

• LESSON TWO: TEMPTED TO SETTLE

Read Exodus 16. Like Israel's captivity in Egypt, our circumstances may not be ideal, but when they're all we know they become our normal. I wish I could say that after the incredible way the Israelites were delivered from the Egyptians through the parting of the Red Sea, their doubts disappeared. But what you'll find in their story is sweetened memories of their slave life in Egypt after momentary discomfort in the desert. After their dramatic rescue, they quickly began to grumble, misremember, and tell embellished tales of their home in Egypt.

> **"Would that we had died by the hand of the Lord in the land of Egypt, when we sat by the meat pots and ate bread to the full, for you have brought us out into this wilderness to kill this whole assembly with hunger."**
>
> **Exodus 16:3 ESV**

Israel may have heard stories about the home God promised, but all they knew themselves was slavery. And they may have even wondered if those stories were true. Facing their Red Sea moment, they would have chosen going back to slavery in Egypt over the unknown. And in their search for water and food after crossing the Red Sea, they would have chosen the meat pots and bread of their slavery too. In the face of doubt, slavery became preferable to freedom. And they were tempted to settle.

Begin with prayer. Ask God to show you how you've been tempted to settle in your own life, how you've been paralyzed by doubt and fear, and how you've chosen captivity to something else over freedom in him. Maybe this looks like being indecisive or procrastinating on a major decision, choosing the safe route instead of the path you sense God asking you to take, or staying in a situation—a relationship, a job, a household, a way of life—that makes you feel constrained instead of stepping into the freedom of another opportunity God brings your way. If you like writing out your prayers, use the space provided below:

Reflect on God's Word. Take time to read 2 Corinthians 3:17. Make this verse your prayer for a few quiet moments.

> **"Now the Lord is the Spirit, and where the Spirit of the Lord is, there is freedom."**
> **2 Corinthians 3:17 NIV**

After a few moments of prayer, write down two or three specific situations or circumstances in your life where you feel, or have felt in the past, like God was distant from you and you doubted his promises or his plan for you. For each area, answer these questions:

- What normal patterns have you been unwilling to release?
- Are you remaining in an unhealthy relationship or situation out of comfort or convenience?
- How have you been allowing areas of complacency or sin to remain simply because they've been normalized?

- In what ways are you partaking in things that are normal for the people around you, when you know God's been calling you to something different?

Think about specific responses and actions when you've been tempted to settle for less than God's best. Ponder the settling actions or patterns God is asking you to give up so he can fulfill his promises to you.

SITUATION ONE:

SITUATION TWO:

SITUATION THREE:

Identify one specific action step you will take today or this week to stop settling for less than God's best and start following God.

MY ACTION GOAL:

In the Exodus story, we see that the human heart has a difficult time leaving normal, if for no other reason than simply because it is familiar.

• LESSON THREE: FINDING THE HEART OF GOD

Our hearts are drawn to security and stability, for *shalom*. That explains why we have a hard time moving away from it. And when we are forced to do so, we get desperate. So did the Israelites. They were desperate for their slavery in Egypt to end, and throughout their wilderness journey, they were desperate for God to continue rescuing them, providing for them, and seeing them. Every time God responds to the Israelites, we catch a glimpse of his heart toward them. God heard the cries of his people. He saw their need for rescue and cared about their longing for a true home. Though Israel may have felt forgotten, God remembered them. In doing so, "he repeats his acts of saving grace towards his people again and again, and in this way fulfills his promises, and shows his own self-consistency" (R. Alan Cole, *Exodus*, Tyndale Old Testament Commentaries, 28).

God is always moved by the broken hearts of his people because that's who God is. God responds with compassion because he *is* compassion; God initiates rescue because God is *the* Rescuer. It's impossible for him to respond in a way that's inconsistent with his own character. And this is the heart of God. As followers of Jesus, we are the modern-day Israelites who have God's attention and God's heart. May we seek to find the heart of God beyond our own desire for security and stability, as he seeks to guide us toward heavenly *shalom*.

Answer the following questions as you consider God's heart toward his people:

- **Read Exodus 2:23–25** and consider how the Israelites were feeling before their exodus from Egypt. What were their prayers like? Has there ever been a time in your life when your prayers were like that too? If so, what were the circumstances?

- **Read Exodus 3.** What reason does God give for sending Moses back to Egypt? What do you notice about God's heart in this passage? How has God also recognized your pain and suffering?

- **Read Exodus 13.** What does God's command to "consecrate every firstborn" (verse 2 NIV) tell us about God's heart toward the Israelites? How does this sort of remembrance help to guide the heart of God's people? Are there moments of remembering in your own life that help to keep your heart open toward God?

God heard the cries of his people, saw their need for rescue, and cared about their longing for a true home. Though Israel may have felt forgotten, God remembered them.

• *LESSON FOUR: UNWELCOMED DETOURS*

It's easy to think that if we step forward in obedience to God, then we will be showered with blessings every step of the journey. Yet the leaving of something is rarely painless, even if it's the right thing. And that's where the Israelites found themselves. They made the decision to leave Egypt and obediently follow God through the wilderness, but their desert circumstances actually weakened their view of God. They forgot God's promise of faithfulness in the midst of what seemed like an unwelcome detour. And despite God's show of power, the Israelites doubted God's promise to bring them home safely. "*It would have been better for us to serve the Egyptians in the wilderness than to die in the wilderness*" (Exodus 14:12 NIV). But the Israelites weren't the only ones with an unwelcome detour. Again, consider the lives of Mary, Hagar, and Ruth. Even Jesus experienced a series of unwelcomed detours as he was tempted, betrayed, beaten, and crucified. And yet God fulfilled his promises time and again in these stories of unwelcomed detours throughout Scripture.

Reflect on these reminders of God's promises in the midst of unknown journeys and unwelcome detours:

> "Now I am about to go the way of all the earth. You know with all your heart and soul that not one of all the good promises the LORD your God gave you has failed. Every promise has been fulfilled; not one has failed."
>
> **Joshua 23:14 NIV**

> "'For I know the plans I have for you,' declares the Lord, 'plans to prosper you and not to harm you, plans to give you hope and a future. Then you will call on me and come and pray to me, and I will listen to you. You will seek me and find me when you seek me with all your heart. I will be found by you,' declares the Lord, 'and will bring you back from captivity. I will gather you from all the nations and places where I have banished you,' declares the Lord, 'and will bring you back to the place from which I carried you into exile.'"
>
> **Jeremiah 29:11–14 NIV**

> "For no matter how many promises God has made, they are 'Yes' in Christ. And so through him the 'Amen' is spoken by us to the glory of God."
>
> **2 Corinthians 1:20 NIV**

Name some of the unwelcomed detours of your life. In what ways have you responded in fear when things didn't go the way you anticipated? What reminds you to lift your eyes to God and pay attention to what God is about to do in the midst of unknown or uncertain circumstances?

Just because we answer God's nudge to move out from our comfort zone doesn't mean the journey will be easy.

• LESSON FIVE: FINDING HOME

The nation of Israel would eventually come to realize that their dwelling place wasn't a destination, but the actual, constant presence of a faithful God. When the Israelites stood on the shore of the Red Sea, murmuring and complaining, wishing they could go back to slavery in Egypt, God showed them a different way. He parted the Red Sea so they could cross on dry land. When the Israelites doubted, God delivered. When they strayed in their hearts, God's heart remained faithful and true.

Much later, Moses would look back with clarity on these events and the years of wilderness wandering that followed. Long after the burning bush, the showdown with Pharaoh, and the decades of nomadic living on the way to the promised land, Moses would pen a prayer of praise. And he concluded that God was their dwelling place, their home, all along. He basically acknowledged to God, *You were always and forever will be home to your people, no matter our geographical location*

These words mean something important for us too. Seeing God as our home means we no longer let our routines, the status quo of those around us, or the patterns handed down to us by our family of origin dictate our comfort or stand in the way of following God's lead. We can throw normal to the wind because our home is a person, not a place. Our home is in a person who has no beginning and no end.

Read this psalm penned by Moses as a prayer of praise:

> **"Lord, you have been our dwelling place**
> **throughout all generations.**
> **Before the mountains were born**
> **or you brought forth the whole world,**
> **from everlasting to everlasting you are God.**

You turn people back to dust,
    saying, 'Return to dust, you mortals.'
A thousand years in your sight
    are like a day that has just gone by,
    or like a watch in the night.
Yet you sweep people away in the sleep of death—
    they are like the new grass of the morning:
In the morning it springs up new,
    but by evening it is dry and withered.

We are consumed by your anger
    and terrified by your indignation.
You have set our iniquities before you,
    our secret sins in the light of your presence.
All our days pass away under your wrath;
    we finish our years with a moan.
Our days may come to seventy years,
    or eighty, if our strength endures;
yet the best of them are but trouble and sorrow,
    for they quickly pass, and we fly away.
If only we knew the power of your anger!
Your wrath is as great as the fear that is your due.
Teach us to number our days,
    that we may gain a heart of wisdom.

Relent, Lord! How long will it be?
    Have compassion on your servants.
Satisfy us in the morning with your unfailing love,
    that we may sing for joy and be glad all our days.
Make us glad for as many days as you have afflicted us,
    for as many years as we have seen trouble.
May your deeds be shown to your servants,
    your splendor to their children.

May the favor of the Lord our God rest on us;
    establish the work of our hands for us—
    yes, establish the work of our hands."

Psalm 90 NIV

Perhaps God has called you out from the familiar by physically displacing you; he's called you from the place you thought of as "home" to a new place of residence. This may be hard at first, but when we make God our dwelling place, we can accept whatever earthly home or new circumstances to which he calls us.

- How have you been like the Israelites, displaced and standing on the shore of the Red Sea wondering how you're ever going to get to safety or experience the comfort of "home" again?

- **Read Mark 10:17–29.** In what ways has God called you to leave something behind, even when the final destination is unknown?

- **Read Matthew 4:18–20.** How did the disciples find their home in Jesus? What did their decision cost them? What does your decision to follow God cost you?

- Like Moses, how have you found your home in God?

Pray for courage to embrace your faith and let go of the familiar as you allow God to be your home. Doing so will prepare you to follow God's journey above your own desires for a particular destination.

God cares too much to leave us standing on shifting sand when he rescued us from the dominion of darkness to stand on the only sure foundation: himself.

• BONUS: INSPIRING STORIES

Read the story of the Roland family at the end of chapter 3 in the book, So Long, Normal.

What inspires you about the story of the Roland family?

In what ways do you sense God asking you to let go and step out in faith as they did?

What specific action step will you take today to step out in faith and follow God?

RECOMMENDED READING

As you reflect on what God is teaching you through this session, you may want to read chapter 3 of *So Long, Normal* by Laura Story. And consider reading chapters 4–7 as you get ready for the next session.

SESSION

3

So Long, Self

GROUP STUDY

INTRODUCTION

Leader, read this section aloud to the group:

As we consider saying goodbye to normal, let's be honest, there is nothing more normal than putting ourselves first in almost everything we do. Whether it's choosing what to have for dinner, agreeing on what movie to watch or playlist to listen to, or thinking our schedule is more important than everyone else stuck in the same rush-hour traffic. Thinking of ourselves first is so ingrained in us, you may even say we were born with it. And perhaps that's true.

We saw how things began to unravel in the story of the Garden in the early chapters of Genesis. And what happened there continues to play out in our lives today. Adam and Eve doubted God, wondering if he was holding out on them, and, thanks to advice from the serpent, took matters into their own hands. They did what was best for themselves. And we've perpetuated that self-focused action ever since.

As a result of our obsession with ourselves, or what's best for our own lives, many of us have lost our contentment in life. We've pursued self-satisfaction because we lost sight of a simple understanding of the gospel of grace found in the good news of Jesus—the gospel which points to

Christ's deep love for us. Instead, our affections have been captured by illusions of success, fame, or financial security. We settle for the contentment we find in these illusions. But to fully realize a life of contentment, we need to say goodbye to self and goodbye to all of our own efforts to earn righteousness (right standing) with God. When we say so long, self, we pursue righteousness because God has loved us and saved us, not because we need to earn his favor. And what a wonderful place this is to be!

While the world and our human nature compel us to focus on ourselves, to strive for acceptance and satisfaction by becoming good enough, strong enough, smart enough, and successful enough, Jesus offers another way. The good news of the gospel means that we can say so long to our obsession with self. And in doing so, we find our true identity as children of God. Truth is, God is crazy about you and there's no amount of goodness or badness that would change that.

As we seek to say goodbye to normal and to the expectations we hold for our lives, our families, and our future, we may not be ready to sing a happy song just yet. But thankfully the Lord says *he* will turn our mourning into dancing (Lamentations 5:15; see also Psalm 30:11). Our role is simply to take the next step in front of us, asking God to turn any self-focus or disappointed expectations into a deeper identity and greater expectation of what he will do in and through us.

So, let's do this together. Let's say so long to our misguided sense of self, and to the expectations that go along with it, and ask God for fresh eyes and fresh faith to expect greater things to come. Greater things found in him. As you learn to let go of yourself, may you hear the beautiful truth of who God says you are in him. And may you learn to walk in it boldly every day.

> **And I pray that you, being rooted and established in love, may have power, together with all the Lord's holy people, to grasp how wide and long and high and deep is the love of Christ.**
>
> **Ephesians 3:17–18 NIV)**

MEMORY VERSE FROM LAST SESSION

Memorizing Scripture is a helpful habit as you learn to say so long to normal. Repeat last week's memory verse out loud as a group.

> "Truly he is my rock and my salvation;
> he is my fortress, I will not be shaken."
>
> **Psalm 62:3 NIV**

TALK ABOUT IT

Take 10–15 minutes to respond to the opening message from Laura. Then take turns answering the following questions in preparation for the video teaching. Use this section each week to get your hearts and minds focused and ready for Laura's teaching.

- Tell us something about yourself that we may not know about you, perhaps something you love or a favorite activity.

—*or*—

- What is your favorite moment from this past year?

> *Our human nature nudges all of us toward the desires of our hearts to some extent. But Jesus is not the means to our ends.*

WATCH VIDEO SESSION THREE (22 MINUTES)

Use the video streaming access code on the inside of the front cover of your study guide or use the DVD to watch this session.

• VIDEO TEACHING NOTES

As you watch the video teaching for this session, use the following outline to record anything that stands out to you.

A few favorite things

Biggest fan and worst critic

> *Self-focus and self-advancements are the very foundation of the elusive American dream.*

Feeling fulfilled

> *Our desire for affirmation and for validation for self isn't wrong, it's just often misplaced.*

Saying so long to self

The gospel: the good news of Jesus

Galatians 2:20

For Paul, *crucified* means "to be put to death"

Crucified with Christ

— Dying to our old selves

— New life in Christ

Psalm 139:13–14

Be like Jesus (Philippians 2:3–8)

— Count: count others as more significant than yourself

— Look: look to the interest of others, not just your own interests

— Think: we have to think with the mind of Jesus

The posture of Jesus

— He emptied himself

— He took on the nature of a servant

— He humbled himself

— He became obedient to a criminal's death

Gratitude and longing

Don't just tell people the gospel, show them.

Show others the gospel

2 Corinthians 5:21

New life = righteousness of God as a child of God

Jesus took on the penalty that our imperfect lives had earned us, that we might receive the blessing that his perfect life had earned him.

• GROUP DISCUSSION

Read each question and take time for group members to give honest and thoughtful responses.

1. How can you relate to Laura's story about the tension she felt with her coworker? Is there a particular situation or scenario in which you counted yourself as more significant than someone else?

2. How does your "self" get in your own way? How have you struggled to put others above yourself?

Saying goodbye to an old way of life can be painful, but our goal is new life, new freedom, and greater purpose and joy.

Select volunteers to read the following passages aloud to the group and discuss the questions with each:

Galatians 2:15–21 NIV

3. According to Laura's teaching, what does Paul mean when he says he's been "crucified with Christ"?

4. What choices, actions, or ways of living have had to be put to death in your life as a result of saying yes to Jesus and being crucified with Christ?

The gospel is the only scenario in which our verdict comes in before our performance.

Select a group member to read this passage out loud:

Philippians 2:1–11

5. How does Paul describe our "new life" in God? How did Jesus demonstrate these characteristics and attributes? Give specific examples.

6. Which characteristic do you struggle with, and why? How can you follow Jesus' example?

Your significance and value is not found in your performance. It's found in Jesus.

Select a group member to read this passage out loud:

2 Corinthians 5:17–21 NIV

7. What does Paul mean when he says we are "Christ's ambassadors" (verse 20)? How can you be more aware of this in the way you live your life?

8. How does saying so long to self make us better ambassadors of Christ and better examples of the gospel or "good news" of Jesus?

What freedom comes when we learn to say so long to self, to striving to be good enough for his love, and when we simply accept the free gift of eternal acceptance that comes through the work of Jesus.

MEMORY VERSE:

Commit this verse to memory this week:

> **"Therefore, if anyone is in Christ, the new creation has come: The old has gone, the new is here!"**
>
> **2 Corinthians 5:17 NIV**

CLOSING PRAYER

Spend time in your group praying in some of the following directions:

- Pray for your group members as they seek to let go of themselves and let God reign in their lives.
- Ask the Holy Spirit to help you understand what it means to be "crucified with Christ"—to die to your old self and find joy in your new life in Christ Jesus.
- Thank God for how he loves you and makes you new, not just once but every day.
- Celebrate the fact that God has given you access to the same humble, servant-hearted posture as Jesus. And pray for opportunities to live that way in your daily life.

Record prayer requests here for easy reference to pray for one another throughout the week:

SESSION

3

So Long, Self

BETWEEN-SESSIONS PERSONAL BIBLE STUDY

Before your next group meeting, spend time with the following five Bible study lessons. Do as much as you have time for, but make it a priority to engage the Scripture a few minutes each day.

• LESSON ONE: YOUR SENSE OF SELF

Read 2 Corinthians 5:14–15 and Hebrews 13:5–6. Most of us wear things, say things, and do things in an effort to manage others' opinions. We all care about our identity—our sense of self. Caring about how others view us isn't especially wrong. But when the perception of others begins to rule our lives or we find ourselves compelled to keep up a certain image, we've been set up for failure. But what does it look like tangibly to not be defined by our roles in life, even the good ones? How can we be free from caring what others think? How do we get to such a liberating place to live? By finding our sense of self in God, not actually in ourselves.

I know, it sounds counterintuitive, but it's the reality of the *Imago Dei*—the reality of having been created in the image of God. We find our sense of self when we lose our sense of self in God. That's right, we have to lose it to find it. We'll talk a little more about this sense of self in lesson 3, but a sense of self basically means your identity—your distinguishing character or individual personality. And it's amazing how much time and money we spend over a lifetime trying to maintain it, alter it, or improve it. We determine our sense of self by how others perceive us, or how we view ourselves, rather than how God views us, the very God who created us in his image.

If we want to say so long to our negative, ever-changing, inward-focused sense of self, then we must embrace our identity in Christ. We must embrace our God-given sense of self and stop the swing between not measuring up and elevating ourselves as the most important. Jesus bore the weight of our sin and shame on the cross so we could walk in confidence and freedom. All we need to do is trust God and cooperate with him, and he will transform our lives and our sense of self from the inside out.

Journal your answers to these questions:

- How is it that we have become so focused on ourselves? What is it about human nature that causes us to be so obsessed with other peoples' perceptions of us?

- In what ways do you put yourself first? Maybe you've ordered your life based on an elevated view of self, or maybe it's the opposite and your deflated view of self is what paralyzes you. Take an honest assessment of the rhythm or routine of your daily life.

- How have you given extra help, resources, or finances *after* first gaining, taking, or securing something for yourself? Name a time when you did just the opposite, given to someone else even when you had needs of your own. How did that make you feel?

- Why is it so hard for you to let go and say so long to yourself? What are you afraid of losing? What are you afraid of finding?

- How does God's love compel you to live for him? How does God help us live for him?

> *"The essence of gospel humility is not thinking more of myself or thinking less of myself, it is thinking of myself less."*
> *—Timothy Keller*

• LESSON TWO: SACRED QUESTIONS AND HONEST ANSWERS

Read Genesis 16. This is the story of Hagar. While we've previously discussed some of her story, I want you to pay attention not to Hagar but to God as he appears to Hagar as the "angel of the Lord." And here's the crux of the story: when God's representatives proved unfaithful (in this case, Abram), God showed up. And he didn't just show up with his presence, he showed up in pursuit. He showed up and asked Hagar,

> **"Where have you come from and where are you going?"**
> **Exodus 16:7 ESV**

Here's an easy tip to remember when studying the Bible: whenever the all-knowing, all-present, and all-powerful God asked someone where they were, where they were going, or where they have been, he was probably not inquiring about their location. He was asking a thoughtful, rhetorical question to engage the person's heart and mind in a moment of need. When God asked a question, it had an intended outcome. Remember when Adam and Eve were hiding and God asked them, "*Where are you?*" (Genesis 3:9). Or when Jesus asked his disciples what they were discussing just so they would have to say it out loud and hear how ridiculous it sounded (Mark 9:33–34). Or when Jesus asked blind Bartimaeus, "*What do you want me to do for you?*" (Mark 10:51). These sacred questions are meant to pierce our self-focused search for truth and identity as we turn to God with honest answers.

Begin with prayer. Ask God to show you how you've been tempted to focus on yourself in your search for truth and identity rather than on his promises. Imagine God walking with you or sitting across the table from you and asking, "*Where are you?*" and "*What do you want?*" How would you honestly answer those questions right now? If you like writing out your prayers, use the space provided below:

Reflect on God's Word. Take time to read Mark 10:35–52. Make this verse your prayer for a few quiet moments.

> **"Go," said Jesus, "your faith has healed you."**
> **Mark 10:52 NIV**

After a few moments of prayer, write down two or three specific scenarios in your life where you have attempted to rely solely on yourself rather than on God. For each area, answer these questions:

- What was I trying to control on my own?
- Why was I doing it without God?

- Was there anything I was trying to hide?
- What did I really want?

Think about specific ways you could ask for God's help in these scenarios. Then pray again and ask God to meet you at your point of need. Be honest with yourself when you're tempted to rely on your own sense of self again.

SCENARIO ONE:

SCENARIO TWO:

SCENARIO THREE:

Identify one specific action step you will take today or this week to stop relying on yourself and start relying on God.

MY ACTION GOAL:

God wants us to consider where we've been and where we're going. He wants us to look at our story and acknowledge our current identity.

• LESSON THREE: REDISCOVERING YOUR IDENTITY

I'll never forget the time a coworker told me I was "exhausting." I took his offhanded comment—which, honestly, was a pretty fair assessment of my behavior—and did two things with it. First, I changed it from a comment on my *behavior* to a description of my *identity*. Then I made it a *label* and attached it to my person, as surely as I might attach a brooch to a sweater. I allowed it to move from the way someone experienced me in a particular moment, on a particular topic, on a specific day, to a defining characteristic of my identity. And I wonder how many times you have done the same thing too. "Hi, I'm Laura and I'm exhausting." I've said this over in my head at least a thousand times. What do you hear in your own head? "Hi, I'm [insert your name here] and I'm . . . *divorced, infertile, anxious, an adulterer, an addict, overweight, not good enough,*" and so on. Or for others, we use our success or fame to push down the negativity and we respond by saying "Hi, I'm [name] and I'm . . . *the CEO, the most popular person at school, the one everyone goes to for help, the best at what I do,*" and you get the idea.

When we allow ourselves to become defined by our pains or our pleasure, our failures or our achievements, we commit a crime against ourselves: *identity theft*. Just because you are divorced or struggling with an addiction doesn't make it your identity. Sure, it's a painful part of your story, but it doesn't define you. You and I are not the sum of our worst mistakes or our greatest accomplishments. Our identity is in Christ—not our sin, our past, our best or worst decisions. Not in what we think of ourselves or who others say we are. You are a new creation in Christ Jesus, and a child of God—*this* is your identity.

Answer the following questions as you rediscover your identity in Jesus:

- **Read Galatians 3:23–29.** How did Jesus change the identity of the people of God? What does this mean for you? How has Jesus changed your identity too?

- **Read Ephesians 2:10–22 NIV.** According to Paul, our identity is found in God's handiwork. How does your true identity in God reflect the handiwork of God? What other metaphors does Paul use to define our identity in Christ? Which one do you identify with the most, and why?

- **Read 2 Corinthians 5:17–21** again and consider how Paul defines our identity in Christ. What does it mean to be a modern-day ambassador of Christ? What do you need to leave behind in order to live like an ambassador of Christ?

To believe our value is based on our behavior is to call God a liar. We must trust who Christ says we are.

LESSON FOUR: MANAGING OUR EXPECTATIONS

In chapter 6 of *So Long, Normal* I tell the story of the first time I took my kids fishing. I go into more detail in the book, but for time's sake, their varied responses and enjoyment level of this activity boiled down to one thing: expectations. The fact that my children had never been fishing before; they had no grid for understanding that you can sit out in the hot sun all day, tirelessly holding this fiberglass fishing rod and walk away with absolutely nothing to show for it.

It made me think about how many times each of us has different expectations for our lives. In fact, much of life's enjoyment relies on correct expectations: expectations about the places we stay, the restaurants we visit, the way others respond to us, the way we respond to others, and so on. We have external expectations of how things should go as well as internal expectations of how things should feel. We *expect* the job or neighborhood, or spouse, or child to meet our dreams, yet find them unfulfilling. We also battle our expectations of ourselves and the expectations others place on us. If we dig deep enough, we even discover that we have expectations of God. When God lives up to our expectations, we thrive, and when he doesn't, we seem disillusioned. Our expectations of God can make or break our spiritual lives.

Now, hear me out, it's not wrong to have expectations. But we may find at times that the healthy thing to do is to say goodbye to our expectations of what's normal. And we do this, in a sense, by faith. We do this by believing in faith that God has a plan that's even better than our best expectations.

Reflect on these reminders of God's faith-filled promises in the midst of our unmet expectations:

> **"'Have faith in God,' Jesus answered. 'Truly I tell you, if anyone says to this mountain, "Go, throw yourself into the sea," and does not doubt in their heart but believes that what they say will happen, it will be done for them. Therefore I tell you, whatever you ask for in prayer, believe that you have received it, and it will be yours.'"**
>
> **Mark 11:22–24 NIV**

> **"Now faith is confidence in what we hope for and assurance about what we do not see. This is what the ancients were commended for. By faith we understand that the universe was formed at God's command, so that what is seen was not made out of what was visible. And without faith it is impossible to please God, because anyone who comes to him must believe that he exists and that he rewards those who earnestly seek him."**
>
> **Hebrews 11:1–3, 6 NIV**

> **"If any of you lacks wisdom, you should ask God, who gives generously to all without finding fault, and it will be given to you. But when you ask, you must believe and not doubt, because the one who doubts is like a wave of the**

> **sea, blown and tossed by the wind. That person should not expect to receive anything from the Lord. Such a person is double-minded and unstable in all they do."**
>
> **James 1:5–8 NIV**

Name some of the unmet expectations of your life. How did you respond to those situations? In what ways did those disappointments affect your faith in God? Which expectations has God met for you lately, and how has this deepened your faith? How might you have faith that God has a plan even better than your expectations?

> *Our role simply is to take the next step in front of us, asking God to turn any disappointed expectations into a greater expectation of what he will do in and through us.*

• *LESSON FIVE: SECURITY*

Can I let you in on a little secret? I struggle with feeling insecure. Despite a fairly mature faith, I still become anxious about the future, especially when it comes to my family. I struggle with whether or not we will be able to provide for them the way we want to, or whether I'll have the wisdom to be the kind of parent my kids need me to be. I get anxious about little things, wondering if and when they'll turn into big things. I wonder if a child's allergy will grow more threatening over time, or how much damage a small roof leak could do to our home, or if the tiny bug on the windowsill means an infestation of termites chewing up our walls. See what I mean? And my insecurity leads me straight to anxiety. This fear and insecurity is a daily battle for me, one I wish would go away with one small prayer, but it's not that simple for me.

By now we've all realized some things—rhythms of life, bad habits, or self-centered patterns—will make a speedy exit from our lives as soon as we acknowledge their presence. But there will be other goodbyes that are more drawn out, more labor-intensive, maybe even more gradual. If you feel stuck at this point or you're still reluctant to leave normal by saying so long to yourself, you're not alone. Trust me. Often our one-time decision to change a habit, shift a perspective, or offer forgiveness has to be bolstered by a thousand daily choices to live out those changes. And it's because as we say so long to normal and to our self, we say so long to a sense of security too.

But know this, God is never in a hurry, and most of his best works are long works. So don't worry if these new ways of learning to let go take practice. Saying goodbye to what we're used to, what feels or seems most secure, is *hard*. But God has infinitely better things in store for you—a new season filled with new opportunities if you're willing to say so long to security in ourselves and locate a new source of security in God.

Read these words of Jesus as he talks about our heavenly Father as our sense of security:

> **"Therefore I tell you, do not worry about your life, what you will eat or drink; or about your body, what you will wear. Is not life more than food, and the body more than clothes? Look at the birds of the air; they do not sow or reap or store away in barns, and yet your heavenly Father feeds them. Are you not much more valuable than they? Can any one of you by worrying add a single hour to your life? And why do you worry about clothes? See how the flowers of the field grow. They do not labor or spin. Yet I tell you that not even Solomon in all his splendor was dressed like one of these. If that is how God clothes the grass of the field, which is here today and tomorrow is thrown into the fire, will he not much more clothe you—you of little faith? So do not worry, saying, 'What shall we eat?' or 'What shall we drink?' or 'What shall we wear?' For the pagans run after all these things, and your heavenly Father knows that you need them. But seek first his kingdom and his righteousness, and all these things will be given to you as well. Therefore do not worry about tomorrow, for tomorrow will worry about itself. Each day has enough trouble of its own."**
>
> **Matthew 6:25–34 NIV**

Now journal your answers to these questions:

- What causes you the most amount of worry and anxiety? On the flip side, what gives you the greatest sense of security?

- **Read Philippians 4:4–9.** According to this passage, how are we supposed to respond to our fear, anxiety, and worry? And how will God respond? In what ways has this been true in God's response to you?

- **Read 2 Timothy 1:7 NIV.** How does knowing you've been given power, love, and self-discipline change the way you cling to whatever currently gives you a sense of security? What do you need to let go of to trust in God and cling to him for your security?

- **Read Psalm 23.** Allow David's beloved words to wash over your soul and cleanse you from your anxiety, fear, and desperate search for your own sense of security. How does this passage remind you of God's faithfulness and dependability?

- Pray for eyes to see the finished work of Christ in the gospel, saying so long to the security this world can only pretend to offer, and instead of trusting yourself, trust the wealth and provision of a loving Father. As you do this, you will find yourself saying so long to normal as you are transformed step by step in God's love.

Worry is the byproduct of insecurity, something God's children never have to dread as we are always being held securely in his hand.

• BONUS: INSPIRING STORIES

Read the story of Kevin Chung at the end of chapter 5 and the story about the Stacks at the end of chapter 7 in the book So Long, Normal.

- What inspires you about Kevin's story or the story of the Stack family?

- In what ways do you sense God calling you to a place or position that brings up a painful past or a future concern, just like Kevin? Or how has God used a current situation in your life, just like the Stacks, to make you rely on him for your strength and security?

- What specific action step will you take today to step out into the uncomfortable and unknown to follow God's calling? How will you anchor yourself in the presence of God as you live with strength and commitment in the place God has called you?

RECOMMENDED READING

As you reflect on what God is teaching you through this session, you may want to read chapters 4–7 of *So Long, Normal* by Laura Story. And consider reading chapters 8–10 as you get ready for the next session.

SESSION

4

Hello, New Life

GROUP STUDY

INTRODUCTION

Leader, read this section aloud to the group:

Today we're talking about the new life God invites us into when we're willing to say so long to normal. It's not only a *new* life, it's an *abundant* life. When God calls us to leave the comfort of the familiar it's because he loves us too much to let us settle for normal. Rather than the accumulation of things, the achievement of prominent positions, or the accolades that promised a sense of significance, the abundant life requires emptying ourselves so that we live with the humble posture of a servant. While this may not sound so great at first, as we study God's Word we begin to understand that living the abundant life is far more fulfilling than anything this world has to offer, our only way to find lasting fulfillment this side of heaven. But this new way of life God offers may, at times, feel like a long, hard road, or a strenuous climb on a muddy trail.

I'll never forget the time my husband, Martin, and I had big plans to hike eight miles in the Cohutta wilderness. We were fairly new to long-distance hiking, having just purchased a book of trails near our Georgia home, and a few miles into the hike, we realized that we were unprepared to complete the trail we set out to conquer. By the time the trail crossed a paved road, we were already dehydrated and desperate to head toward home. So we did something we had never done before: we hitchhiked. Hopping in a car with a stranger who promised to take us back to our car seemed like the lesser of two dire outcomes.

Fast-forward a few years and we were with our kids on a strenuous uphill climb, when Ben, one of our twins asked, “Mom, are there any hikes in your hike book that go downhill to get to the top of the mountain?” It was a sweet question, and it gave us all a good laugh. But the answer was *no*, both in hiking and in life. Opening ourselves up to living an abundant life in Christ will require rigorous treks filled with highs and lows. But just because we’re walking a difficult path doesn’t mean we’re on the wrong road. In the kingdom of God, no trial is wasted.

As we wind our way through each turn, each detour, and each trial of our lives, the lessons we learn may be of equal or greater value to God’s heart than the outcome or destination ever was. Following Jesus may mean laying aside our obsession with productivity, efficiency, and timeliness, but trust me, it will all be worth it in the end. In Romans, Paul encouraged his Christian readers amid the trials and tribulations they were facing. He wrote about the hard road God sometimes allows us to walk, because the hard road is the only way to become what God created us to become. The difficult journey is often the means to producing Christ’s character in us so that we might live a new life—an abundant life.

Whether we’re being called to embrace an abundant life where we are or to embrace change in our circumstances, one thing is for sure in this new life: God is always at work. And we can rest assured that he has given us everything we need to make the journey.

The key to living a new life is recognizing you don’t have to have it all figured out. Simply turn toward God and allow him to lead you one step at a time.

MEMORY VERSE FROM LAST SESSION

Memorizing Scripture is a helpful habit as you learn to say so long to normal. Repeat last week's memory verse out loud as a group.

> **Therefore, if anyone is in Christ, the new creation has come: The old has gone, the new is here!**
>
> **2 Corinthians 5:17 NIV**

TALK ABOUT IT

Take 10–15 minutes to respond to the opening message from Laura. Then take turns answering the following questions in preparation for the video teaching. Use this section each week to get your hearts and minds focused and ready for Laura's teaching.

- How's your "so, long" journey going so far?

—or—

- What trial are you facing right now? And have you experienced God's presence amid this trial?

Our hope for the journey is the result of a process of endurance.

WATCH VIDEO SESSION FOUR (21 MINUTES)

Use the video streaming access code on the inside of the front cover of your study guide or use the DVD to watch this session.

• VIDEO TEACHING NOTES

As you watch the video teaching for this session, use the following outline to record anything that stands out to you.

Quick check-in

It's a journey, not a sprint

Philippians 1:6

— The end goal: saying hello to what's next

Stepping out with courage

Living boldly

2 Corinthians 1:20

God's good and meaningful plan for your life

John 10:10

— Abundant life in Christ

— Trials

We unconsciously believe the lie that our main goal in life should be the absence of anything hard.

Happiness vs. holiness (Romans 5:3–5)

— Tethered

A tethered life is a secure life and a sustained life.

— Secure (John 10:27–28

— Sustained (John 15:5)

— Abiding

"Abiding in Him is not a work we have to do as the condition for enjoying His salvation, but a consenting to let Him do all, for us, and in us, and through us. Abiding is a work He does for us—the fruit and the power of His redeeming love. Our part is simply to yield, to trust, and to wait for what He has engaged to perform."

—Andrew Murray, Abide in Christ, *23, 24*

Tremendous

Tremendous: notable by reason of extreme size, power, greatness, or excellence.

The story of George Mueller

Grant us the faith to live boldly,
to ask audaciously, and to see you
do extraordinary things.

• GROUP DISCUSSION

Read each question and take time for group members to give honest and thoughtful responses.

1. What stands out to you about Laura's teaching today? How can you relate to the stories she shared?

2. Can you think of a past or present circumstance that has required you to step out in courage and live boldly? How did it feel to respond this way, and would you be willing to do it again? Why or why not?

Though our trials may be long, we are never left alone in them.

Select volunteers to read the following passages aloud to the group and discuss the questions with each:

Romans 5:1–11 NIV

3. As we learned in Laura's teaching, happiness doesn't necessarily lead to holiness, but holiness often leads to happiness. What else leads to holiness according to this passage? And how have you experienced happiness as a result of holiness?

4. Why is suffering essential on the journey to holiness? How would you define suffering, and in what ways have you suffered as individuals or as a community?

The new life we have in God may be one of the trials, but we will never have to face those trials alone.

Select a group member to read this passage out loud:

John 10:24–38 NIV

5. According to Jesus' description, what are the characteristics of his followers that Jesus likens to sheep? And what kind of security does Jesus provide for his "sheep"? In what ways has Jesus provided security for you?

6. Why do you think it was hard for the disciples to tether themselves to Jesus? What kind of trials did Jesus face, such as the one in this passage, while his disciples were tethered to him? What makes it hard or comforting for you to be tethered to Jesus?

God's mission for our lives is not a solo endeavor embarked upon in our own strength; it's something we do with God. God shoulders the load when our lives are tethered to his.

Select a group member to read this passage out loud:

John 15:1–11 NIV

7. What does Jesus mean when he says, "abide in me" and "abide in my love"? How does this message contribute to the sustained life Laura mentioned in her teaching, and how has this been true for you?

8. Where or how has God begun a good work in you during this Bible study? How does the love of God make it possible for you to say hello to your new normal? Is there any lingering fear or doubt that keeps you from wanting to say so long to normal at this point?

God is always wanting to work through us for the sake of his kingdom.

MEMORY VERSE:

Commit this verse to memory this week:

> **"For I am confident of this very thing, that He who began a good work among you will complete it by the day of Christ Jesus."**
>
> **Philippians 1:6 NASB**

CLOSING PRAYER

Spend time in your group praying in some of the following directions:

- Pray for your group members as they trust the good work God is doing in their lives and start to say hello to their new normal.

- Ask the Holy Spirit to grant you the faith to live boldly, to ask audaciously, and to do extraordinary things.
- Thank God for how he loves you, provides security for you, and sustains you.
- Celebrate the idea of a new normal and a new life in Christ.

Record prayer requests here for easy reference to pray for one another throughout the week:

SESSION

4

Hello, New Life

BETWEEN-SESSIONS PERSONAL BIBLE STUDY

Before your next group meeting, spend time with the following five Bible study lessons. Do as much as you have time for, but make it a priority to engage the Scripture a few minutes each day.

• LESSON ONE: TRIALS

Read Romans 5.

I don't know about you, but my normal response to anything hard is to figure out how to get out of it or go around it. If there's an easier way to fix a leaky shower rather than ripping up the entire tile floor, then I'm all about it. If I can avoid apologizing to the person I've offended and ease my way around the situation, I'm all in. If I can somehow get out of jury duty with a legitimate, albeit nonurgent, reason, I'm all ears. While we're focused on finding the way out of or around the trial, God is more concerned with how we live by faith *through* it. He knows what's at stake, how the struggle can make us more like Christ, and how the disruptions in our lives can open us up to the new life God offers through Jesus. But going *through* the struggle is the one thing I'd prefer most to avoid.

In Romans 5, Paul refers to the kind of character we develop as a result of going through trials. This kind of character is not possible apart from suffering. Character is hard to come by but may be your most valuable possession. It's the diamond formed from continued heat exposure and pressure of the earth. It's the beautiful canyon cut and forged into the earth by the piercing pressure of roaring waters. This is the character of which Paul speaks. And character can only be gained when we stop getting out of or going around our discomfort and start pressing *through* it. This is not the easy way; rather, it's often the hardest way, and often the only way, into our new life in Christ. But Paul tells us that the reward for our trials, for our suffering, endurance, and gaining this kind of character, is hope.

Journal your answers to these questions:

- What stands out to you about Paul's letter to the Romans? Perhaps something that you didn't notice when you read a few of these verses with the group?

- What trials are you facing right now? And what word would you use to describe each one of these trials? For example, is there a thought, feeling, or sensation that comes to mind as you read over your list?

- When you consider the trials you are facing, it's not wrong as a believer to pray for God's deliverance. But, if God chooses to answer your prayers differently than what you are asking, or to do so in a different time frame than you are asking, how might you still live out your faith *through* the trial?

- In what ways do Paul's words bring comfort to your situation, knowing that suffering produces endurance, endurance produces character, and character produces hope (5:3–5 ESV)? How have you experienced suffering, endurance, character, and hope as a result of your trials? How is suffering shaping you?

- How have your trials caused you to "rejoice in God"? If you haven't considered rejoicing, do so now. What can you celebrate or rejoice about regarding your situation(s)? Sometimes during a trial, the joy comes from noticing how God is shaping your life and how God is present with you amid your hardships.

Endurance and character are works of the Spirit, birthed in our hearts along the road of suffering.

• LESSON TWO: A TETHERED LIFE

Read John 15.

Though the life Jesus calls us to is a life with trials, we are always tethered to him. He will never leave us untethered or tumbling through life with nothing to grab on to. We are always in the arms of our great and mighty God, as long as we're willing to abide in him. Throughout his public ministry, Jesus taught on the importance of staying connected with the Father. Here in the gospel of John, Jesus chose the plant life metaphor to illustrate how we are forever connected to God through himself, and at the same time, called to stay connected by making the intentional choice to stay tethered, or *abide*, in him.

Jesus not only tells us the benefits of abiding in him—the fact that he abides or remains in us too—but he also describes the consequences of *not* abiding in him. Jesus said we cannot bear fruit on our own if we don't abide in him. Imagine a fruitless life, like a tree that's been toppled by a storm, roots unearthed, and unable to access nutrients from the soil to grow the fruit it's meant to grow. These verses in John paint this picture and give the definitive warning,

> **". . . apart from me you can do nothing."**
>
> **John 15:5 ESV**

The good news is: abiding is a work God does for us; it's the fruit and the power of his redeeming love. Our part is simply to yield, to trust, and to stay tethered to Jesus as we wait for what he has promised us. It's through our yielding and trusting and waiting while tethered to Jesus that we begin to flourish. To think of God as the vinedresser in John 15 is to compare him to a caring gardener who plants and cultivates his crops. Not only does God tend to us for our flourishing, he is the very life force that brings about that flourishing. When we abide in God through Christ, his life flows through us and produces fruit.

Begin with prayer. Ask God to show you where you need to say goodbye to many of the places you've been abiding outside of him. In what things of this world do you attempt to seek the nourishment that only God can truly give? What do you need to let go of so you can abide in God? If you like writing out your prayers, use the space provided below:

Reflect on God's Word. Read this verse and make it your prayer for a few quiet moments.

> **"These things I have spoken to you, that my joy may be in you, and that your joy may be full."**
>
> **John 15:11 ESV**

After a few moments of prayer, consider a few specific areas of your life where God is asking you to abide or remain in him and answer these questions:

- Where do I sense God asking me to abide in him, and why?
- What choices do I need to make to start abiding in Jesus?
- What kind of rest comes as a result of abiding in Jesus in these areas—physically, emotionally, mentally, spiritually, relationally?
- In what ways is it possible to flourish in these areas with God?

AREA ONE:

AREA TWO:

AREA THREE:

Identify one specific action step you will take today or this week to stop seeking nourishment and rest from the world and start abiding in God instead.

MY ACTION GOAL:

We are tethered to a faithful God who helps us not only to survive but to thrive.

• LESSON THREE: A TREMENDOUS LIFE

The life we gain in Christ is a tremendous life. Consider the joy of Paul who sang hymns while chained in a dark jail cell, the endurance of Joseph who trusted and obeyed God through every twist and turn of his story, the faith of Noah who built a massive boat when there wasn't a rain cloud in the sky, and the boldness of David who danced half-naked and unashamed as he celebrated the presence of God. When we yield to a new life in Christ and stay tethered to him amid our trials, we exchange a normal life for a tremendous life.

When we say goodbye to normal, we embark on an adventure with God that is by no means safe or predictable, but one that starts with an extraordinary journey of faith; a journey that begins quietly inside each of our hearts. Here's something I want you to hear loud and clear: the tremendous life isn't always a result of us leaving something or going somewhere. The tremendous life is sometimes *staying*. Sometimes, it is asking God for eyes to see the needs right in front of us and responding to those needs in courage.

Answer the following questions as you consider God's invitation to you to live a tremendous life:

- **Read Hebrews 11.** How did the people mentioned in this passage live a tremendous life as a result of their faith? Which individual sticks out to you, and why?

- **Read Acts 16:16–40.** How did Paul and Silas respond with extraordinary faith? Based on what you know about their lives in the remainder of the New Testament, how did this experience allow these men to live tremendous lives?

- **Read 2 Samuel 6:1–15** and consider how David's extraordinary faith as a leader led to a tremendous, albeit at times, troubled life. What does it mean to you to know that David lived both a tremendous *and* troubled life? How has the same been true for you?

- **Take a pulse.** Does the invitation to live a tremendous life mean God is asking you to *stay* and have the courage to respond to the needs right in front of you, or *leave* and pursue the next place where God is calling you? What are you thinking, sensing, or feeling as you consider God's invitation to you?

The potential of our lives is boundless when we abide in Christ, living the tremendous life of a child of God.

• LESSON FOUR: A NEW LENS ON LIFE

With our new life in Christ, it should be of no surprise to us that Jesus came not just to change who we are but how we see things. Because of Jesus, you and I now have a new lens through which to view ourselves, others, and the world. Saying so long to normal and hello to new life in Christ is one of those life-changing encounters that change the entirety of our perspective.

But it's not enough to simply say hello to the new life God gives us; we must embrace our new vision which changes the way we see ourselves. In doing so, we learn to see ourselves as more, and simultaneously, as less. We are made more as sons and daughters of God, and we are made less as we learn to recognize that every ability we have and every possession we own has been claimed and enlisted for a greater cause than ourselves.

In Christ, our old ways must die and our new ways must be guided by the Spirit. We are fully his. We also learn to see others as image bearers of God. This is the great turning point for our hearts: seeing the *Imago Dei* in every life at every age. As we say hello to a new vision, this vision changes the way we see ourselves and the way we see the world. We are no longer our own and we see each life around us as created in God's image.

Reflect on these reminders of God's love in our new life in Christ:

> **"See what great love the Father has lavished on us, that we should be called children of God! And that is what we are! The reason the world does not know us is that it did not know him. Dear friends, now we are children of God, and what we will be has not yet been made known. But we know that when Christ appears, we shall be like him, for we shall see him as he is. All who have this hope in him purify themselves, just as he is pure."**
>
> **1 John 3:1–3 NIV**

> **"Because you are his sons, God sent the Spirit of his Son into our hearts, the Spirit who calls out, 'Abba, Father.' So you are no longer a slave, but God's child; and since you are his child, God has made you also an heir."**
>
> **Galatians 4:6–7 NIV**

> **"You are no longer foreigners and strangers, but fellow citizens with God's people and also members of his household, built on the foundation of the apostles and prophets, with Christ Jesus himself as the chief cornerstone. In him the whole building is joined together and rises to become a holy temple in the Lord. And in him you too are being built together to become a dwelling in which God lives by his Spirit."**
>
> **Ephesians 2:19–22 NIV**

Name some of the ways these passages describe us before our new life in Christ. What words would you use to describe how it feels to be called a son or daughter of God? How does this change the way you interact with

God? How does being a citizen of God's kingdom change the way you live your life and the actions you take in your community?

Before we can consider how we might use our hands and feet, we must embrace God's vision, using our eyes; for the posture of a person ready for mission is one who sees things others might not see.

• LESSON FIVE: A NEW MISSION WITH GOD

As most of you already know, one of the great joys of my life comes from sharing songs and stories that somehow bring hope to people processing how real life and real faith interact. And most often, I get to do this with my family in tow. I have to laugh when people say to me, "Life on the road must be so glamorous!" if only they could see the six of us crammed into a minivan, the upholstery covered in sticky Cheeto dust and the resounding sound of my children asking, "Are we there yet?" But the truth is, I wouldn't trade those moments for anything in the world. From flat tires to 5 a.m. call times, every bit of joy and struggle has been part of the mission to which God has called our family. It has not been normal, but it has been an adventure, for sure.

And it's a reminder that when we say goodbye to normal, we don't just receive a new life; we receive a new mission. By mission, I mean the calling God places on your life. This could be as drastic as moving overseas or as simple as taking time to get to know your neighbors. It's not so much about where you go, but how you live. Living on mission with God means living each moment with gospel purpose. And it will look different for every person based on your abilities, background, resources, and stage of life. But it all starts with a willingness to live out a new life and a new vision as you say hello to a new mission.

Read these words of the apostle Paul who urges fellow believers to live out their new mission:

> **"Therefore, I urge you, brothers and sisters, in view of God's mercy, to offer your bodies as a living sacrifice, holy and pleasing to God—this is your true and proper worship. Do not conform to the pattern of this world, but be transformed by the renewing of your mind. Then you will be able to test and approve what God's will is—his good, pleasing and perfect will. For by the grace given me I say to every one of you: Do not think of yourself more highly than you ought, but rather think of yourself with sober judgment, in accordance with the faith God has distributed to each of you. For just as each of us has one body with many members, and these members do not all have the same function, so in Christ we, though many, form one body, and each member belongs to all the others. We have different gifts, according to the grace given to each of us. If your gift is prophesying, then prophesy in accordance with your faith; if it is serving, then serve; if it is teaching, then teach; if it is to encourage, then give encouragement; if it is giving, then give generously; if it is to lead, do it diligently; if it is to show mercy, do it cheerfully."**
>
> **Romans 12:1–8 NIV**

Now journal your answers to these questions:

- How has God gifted you? How could you use those gifts for gospel purposes?

- Read Acts 1:1–8. What is the mission God is calling you to? Ask for eyes to see and for a heart and mind to consider where you might live out this mission, near or far. Ask God to show you your own Jerusalem (near), Judea (in-between), and Samaria (far), and "ends of the earth."

- Read Hebrews 12:1–3. This passage was written to inspire and encourage our faith for the long haul because the mission God called you to is a journey, not a sprint. And if there's anyone who understands this, it's Jesus. Is there anything hindering or entangling you from making progress on this journey? What do you need to lay down so you can keep moving toward your mission? What might help you keep your eyes fixed on Jesus?

- Read Matthew 11:28–30. Though the mission God calls some to may be difficult, it's never intended to be burdensome. What does Jesus mean when he says, "My yoke is easy, and my burden is light"? How has Jesus made this true for you? How does an "easy yoke" and a "light burden" make it easier to live on mission?

Pray for courage to embrace the idea of being "on mission." Even though mission doesn't always involve a change in geography, it always involves a change. Ask God to show you how living on mission requires adjusting your life, including your time, your money, and your talents. Thank God for the help he provides along the way, and for the inspiring illustrations he gives throughout the Bible of others who have been on mission with him. May you find hope and strength in the stories of people such as Gideon (book of Judges), Isaiah (book of Isaiah), Jeremiah (book of Jeremiah), and in the story of Jesus and his disciples at the time of the Great Commission (book of Matthew).

When you feel like God has called you to something too big, something for which you're not fully equipped, remember the disciples who doubted, yet still went forth to the nations with the gospel message of Jesus in the power of the Holy Spirit.

• BONUS: INSPIRING STORIES

Read the stories of Bailey Moody at the end of chapter 8 and the Cook family at the end of chapter 10 in the book So Long, Normal.

- What inspires you about these stories? Which one resonates most with you, and why?

- Similar to Bailey, in what ways has God done good things *in* you and *through* you even during very challenging circumstances? Or, like the Cook family, how has God used a calling or mission to deepen and strengthen you?

- How have your trials led to new beginnings? How have you had to trust God to show you his greater goodness during a messy or chaotic mission? And moving forward, how will you lean on God and your community in times of need?

RECOMMENDED READING

As you reflect on what God is teaching you through this session, you may want to read chapters 8–10 of *So Long, Normal* by Laura Story. And consider reading chapter 11 as you get ready for the next session.

SESSION

5

Hello, Unknown

GROUP STUDY

INTRODUCTION

Leader, read this section aloud to the group:

Before we go any further, I just want to say thank you for the time you have invested in taking this journey with me. While I may be the author, I am simply another woman seeking to let go of normal, with all its elusiveness, and embrace something more solid and valuable. That's why I pray that even with the silliness of some of my personal stories, you'll have heard from the Lord in his Word, not just from me.

The bottom line as we finish this last session of *So Long, Normal* is this: we are called to say goodbye to what's normal and hello to the unknown. This is often the hardest part of the journey. I wish I could leave you with definitive next steps. I wish I could paint for you a clear picture of what these truths should look like played out in your own life. I wish I could give you details and a framework for the new normal I am challenging you to embrace. But the tricky thing about the future is that most of it is unknown. God has called all of us to step out on a tremendous adventure of faith, and yet, as we saw with the Israelites leaving Egypt, it's often easier to stay put and live a less fulfilling, normal life because it's "safer."

But here's what I've learned from my own experience as well as the experiences of others, especially the stories shared throughout my book. Venturing into the unknown with God *is* the safest place you could possibly be. And isn't that what we're all after anyway? The safest place to be? That's why we cling to normal, and yet God offers us an alternative. He asks us to cling to him as God calls us into the unknown. God is reframing our idea of normal and our experience of comfort and safety if we're willing to let him do so in our lives.

If we belong to Jesus, then every piece of our lives is his. Where he leads, we follow, even when the path is not as clear as we might wish. Such risk-taking often looks foolish to the world, and yet it is an attractive quality of a follower of Christ. And how could we not step out in boldness when our eyes are fixed on Jesus who gave his whole life for us.

Besides, God never sends his children on mission alone. Through Jesus, God provides three great comforts to accompany us on this journey into the unknown. We have a compass to guide us, a community to cheer us on, and a constant source of hope. These comforts are gifts to steady us no matter how perilous the landscape appears.

> *"Wherever He leads, I'll go."*
>
> ***R.S. Jones***

MEMORY VERSE FROM LAST SESSION

Memorizing Scripture is a helpful habit as you learn to say so long to normal. Repeat last week's memory verse out loud as a group.

> **"For I am confident of this very thing, that he who began a good work among you will complete it by the day of Christ Jesus."**
>
> **Philippians 1:6 NASB**

TALK ABOUT IT

Take 10–15 minutes to respond to the opening message from Laura. Then take turns answering the following questions in preparation for the video teaching. Use this section each week to get your hearts and minds focused and ready for Laura's teaching.

- Share one thing that excites you and one thing that scares you about embracing a new chapter of life.

  —or—

- How have you stepped into the unknown before? Briefly share the situation and what prompted you to take that step.

> *Our loss of normal can be a place of expectancy rather than disillusionment.*

WATCH VIDEO SESSION FIVE (23 MINUTES)

Use the video streaming access code on the inside of the front cover of your study guide or use the DVD to watch this session.

• VIDEO TEACHING NOTES

As you watch the video teaching for this session, use the following outline to record anything that stands out to you.

So Long, Normal

Hello, Unknown

My faith has become my steady, and my circumstances no longer have the power to unravel me.

Now what?

> "I keep my eyes on the Lord.
> With him at my right hand, I will not be shaken."
>
> **Psalm 16:8 NIV**

The 3 Cs for the road

If we have the right things for the journey, we can be prepared for anything, and we can face an unknown future boldly.

— A compass

> "Thy word is a lamp unto my feet, and a light unto my path."
> **Psalm 119:105 KJV**

— God's Word as our compass

— Community

> "And they devoted themselves to the apostles' teaching and the fellowship, to the breaking of bread and the prayers. And awe came upon every soul, and many wonders and signs were being done through the apostles. And all who believed were together and had all things in common."
> **Acts 2:42–44 ESV**

> "And they were selling their possessions and belongings and distributing the proceeds to all, as any had need. And day by day, attending the temple together and breaking bread in their homes, they received their food with glad and generous hearts, praising God and having favor with all the people. And the Lord added to their number day by day those who were being saved."
> **Acts 2:45–47 ESV**

Two products of community:

God is doing new things

God is bringing new people

How does the word community make you feel?

To the believer on the inside: just turn around, notice who is standing outside the circle, and invite them in.

Be the friend you've longed for others to be to you.

To the person on the outside: try it again.

> **"Therefore, since we are surrounded by so great a cloud of witnesses, let us also lay aside every weight, and sin which clings so closely, and let us run with endurance the race that is set before us."**
>
> **Hebrews 12:1 ESV**

Constant Companion

> **"Fear not, for I have redeemed you;**
> **I have called you by name, you are mine.**
> **When you pass through the waters, I will be with you;**
> **and through the rivers, they shall not overwhelm you;**
> **when you walk through the fire you shall not be burned,**
> **and the flame shall not consume you.**
> **For I am the Lord your God,**
> **The Holy One of Israel, your Savior."**
>
> **Isaiah 43:1–3 ESV**

FEAR	FAITH
What causes fear?	What does God give us as anecdotes to fear?

To say God is our constant companion doesn't just mean that he's always with you. It means he is also for you.

Change is an opportunity, not an enemy

As you say so long to normal, may you find an exciting adventure of faith, trusting your every unknown to a loving and faithful God.

• GROUP DISCUSSION

Read each question and take time for group members to give honest and thoughtful responses.

1. Let's do a little Bible study recap. How has God shaken what has needed to be shaken in your life? How has God exposed the areas where you needed to loosen your grip on the things of this world? And how have you begun to see change as an opportunity rather than as an enemy?

2. What else stands out to you about Laura's teaching today? What do you hear God saying to you through what she shared?

Taking new steps of faith isn't just about where you're going, it's about being honest with yourself about where you are right now.

Select volunteers to read the following passages aloud to the group and discuss the questions with each:

Psalm 119:97–106 NIV

3. How has God's Word been a compass for your life? How have you heard God speak to you through his Word? Share about a time that a specific verse gave you instruction and guidance in a particular season in your life.

4. Just like God guided the psalmist with his law as a lamp, in what ways do you need or want God to guide you on this journey into the unknown? After listening to Laura, what scares you or excites you the most about this journey?

A compass points north—a fixed point around which every other location is identified. For the believer, this is God and his Word.

Select a group member to read this passage out loud:

Acts 2:37–47 NIV

5. What made community so essential for the early Christians after the death and resurrection of Jesus? Why is community still so essential for us today? How is the true community we see in Scripture different than simply a gathering of people?

6. As Laura encouraged us to consider, do you identify more with the "person on the inside" or the "person on the outside"? And what could you do to befriend someone who is opposite of where you see yourself?

There is comfort in community. It's where we're called to raise our families on mission for God.

Select a group member to read this passage out loud:

Isaiah 43:1–7 NIV

7. The Lord reminded Isaiah of his companionship not just in everyday circumstances, but in some of the most extreme and extraordinary circumstances as well. How does the idea of God as your companion through everything bring comfort to you? What practices can you add to your daily life to remind you of God's closeness?

8. Revisit the Fear and Faith exercise Laura led us through during her teaching. What causes fear for you as you say goodbye to normal and venture into the unknown? And what has God given you as an anecdote or response to that fear? Are you ready to say hello to the unknown?

We can face the unknown future with boldness and joy knowing that we have a God who will never leave or forsake us, and is always working for our good and his greater glory.

MEMORY VERSE:

Commit this verse to memory this week:

"Now to him who is able to do immeasurably more than all we ask or imagine, according to his power that is at work within us, to him be glory in the church and in Christ Jesus throughout all generations, for ever and ever! Amen."

Ephesians 3:20 NIV

CLOSING PRAYER

Spend time in your group praying in some of the following directions:

- Pray for your group members as they trust God with the unknown journey ahead.
- Ask the Holy Spirit to continue to shake what needs to be shaken in your life and expose the areas where you need to loosen your grip on things of this world.
- Thank God for helping you see change as an opportunity rather than as an enemy or a threat.
- Celebrate the hope and joy of the unknown journey ahead as you rest in the safety and comfort of your Creator God.

Record prayer requests here for easy reference to pray for one another throughout the week:

SESSION

5

Hello, Unknown

BETWEEN-SESSIONS PERSONAL BIBLE STUDY

As you conclude, spend time with the following five Bible study lessons. Do as much as you have time for, but make it a priority to engage the Scripture a few minutes each day. In the coming days, get together with one or two members of your group to discuss what you discovered.

• LESSON ONE: OUR COMPASS

Read Psalm 119:9–16, Proverbs 3:5–6, and Hebrews 4.

The purpose of a compass is to show which direction will get us back on course. It simply points to the north—a fixed point in relation to your current location. I'll get straight to the point here: *God is the greatest compass we've ever been given as believers.* And we come to understand God as our compass through his Word.

In the Old Testament, we see God's commitment to the Israelites as his people, and subsequently, the guidance he gives them, physically and spiritually, as the result of his love and loyalty. In the New Testament, God guides his people through the life and teachings of Jesus. Jesus not only gives the Jews new directions for following God, but he gives directions to *all* of God's followers, including us, as he points to love and the pursuit of righteousness as the way to follow God.

But how do we do this? How do we venture into the unknown and embrace a new way of life with God as our compass and our guide? Proverbs 3 gives us a few important clues: *trust in God with all of our hearts, lean not on our own understanding, and submit our ways to him* (NIV). When we follow God's wisdom in his Word, we reap the benefits of venturing with God into the unknown. God's Word shows us how he revives us when we're weary, keeps us steady when we are uncertain, and lights our way so we can see. God is *alive and active* through his Word (Hebrews 4:12 NIV). To embark on a faith journey with God as our compass and his Word as our guide is to start a journey with everything we could ever need, even when we're headed into the unknown. Let me say that again: with God as our compass and his Word as our guide, *you have everything you could ever need.*

Journal your answers to these questions:

- What stands out to you about David's prayer to God in Psalm 119? How does David ensure he stays focused on God has his compass and his guide?

- According to Proverbs 3, the key to experiencing peace on our journey that is life is twofold: trust God and let go of what you know. Like the movement of the compass dial, through the Holy Spirit, God directs us, but we must be willing to move—especially into that which we cannot "see." Describe how you could specifically (1) trust God, (2) lean on him, and (3) submit to him in an area or situation you need to move from right now.

- According to the passage in Hebrews, God's word is *alive* and *active* (verse 12 NIV). What does this mean? How have you experienced

God's Word as active and alive for you and for others in your faith community?

- If God's Word is hidden in our hearts (Psalm 119:11), then God is both an internal (spiritual) *and* external (physical) compass for our lives. How have you sensed God guiding you internally in your spiritual life—using your sense of intuition prompted by the Spirit as you follow him? And how have you seen God guiding you externally in your physical life—using events, experiences, and the encouragement of others as you follow him?

- How does God's Word help you stay connected to God as your compass and your guide? What habits or spiritual disciplines keep you plugged into God as your True North?

God's Word is our constant north in an ever-changing culture and world.

• LESSON TWO: OUR COMMUNITY

Read Ephesians 4. As I reflect on my quirkiness as a middle schooler, I know my desire to be "normal" wasn't a desire just for conformity; deep down, it was a desire for community. If I could only dress like the cool kids, talk like them, look like them, and joke like them, I could be one of them. Or so I thought. If you're like me and simply hearing the word *community* brings up middle-school memories, then the word *community* may need some definition. What I'm referring to here is *biblical community*—the kind of community where bonds run deeper than affinity groups, social clubs, or middle-school memories. It's the kind of community where people from all different walks of life are welcome. There is no uniformity, only the ability to discuss differing views respectfully and without fear of division.

> **"There is one body and one spirit . . ."**
>
> **Ephesians 4:4 ESV**

Biblical community is a powerful way of sharing the gospel message of Jesus with the world, not just some warm, fuzzy element of fellowship. Paul's letter to the Ephesians also tells us how the Holy Spirit gave us the bond of peace as a community, and yet God calls us to foster this peaceful bond by relating to one another with humility, gentleness, and patience.

After the death and resurrection of Jesus, the disciples journeyed into a very real future of unknown. In the midst of processing the past three years of living on mission with Jesus, they now faced life without him. As they huddled together praying and waiting on God for their next step, they had to let go of many religious traditions to which they had held. And they were able to do so and walk into the unknown because they had been given new life, but also because they had each other. The disciples left their normal religious community to find *true* community in their new gospel identity and the new gospel mission. And we have the opportunity to find *true* community too.

Begin with prayer. Ask God to show you which places and people have been this kind of true community for you. How has God called you to live on mission in your community? Or how has God brought community around you in the places where he's called you to be on mission? How do you desire to participate in true biblical community? If you like writing out your prayers, use the space provided below:

Reflect on God's Word. Read this verse and make it your prayer for a few quiet moments.

> **"Be kind and compassionate to one another, forgiving each other, just as in Christ God forgave you."**
>
> **Ephesians 4:32 NIV**

After a few moments of prayer, consider three specific places that represent "community" to you (i.e., your Bible study, your coworkers, fellow school parents, your neighborhood, and so on). Think about how those places reflect the idea of biblical community as you answer these questions:

- Where do I see humility, gentleness, and patience practiced in these places?
- How is space made for respectful discourse even when community members disagree?
- In what ways do these communities reflect the unifying ways of the early church?
- Do you feel the freedom to be vulnerable in that community?

COMMUNITY #1:

COMMUNITY #2:

COMMUNITY #3:

Identify one specific action step you will take today or this week to contribute to the peace and unity of one of the communities. Bonus points if you can think of one action step for all three places that represent community to you!

MY ACTION GOAL:

> *Community may look different than the one we're used to, and that's okay. Remember, we're Christians—different is good!*

• LESSON THREE: OUR COMPANION

Because we know God to be true to his word, we do not need to fear, even when stepping into uncharted territory. We may feel lonely, but we will never be alone. We may be abandoned by or estranged from people who promise to be constant, but our hearts are forever safe in the hands of a loving Father. But God isn't just our loving Father; he's also our constant companion. He was with Paul in every jail cell. He was with Daniel in the lions' den. He was with Jonah in the whale. He was with David, the psalmist, who tells us there is no place we can escape his spirit and nowhere to flee from his presence (Psalm 139:7). He even sealed his commitment to us with the very blood of his Son, Jesus. Even in Jesus' last charge to his disciples, the send-off we refer to as the Great Commission, his final words give the disciples the assurance they need for the daunting task ahead: "And behold, I am with you always, to the end of the age" (Matthew 28:20 ESV). God is our steady, unchanging, faithful, and constant companion.

Answer the following questions as you consider God's invitation to journey with Him into the unknown:

- Are there particular situations or circumstances that cause you to feel lonely? Has there been a relationship in your life where you felt abandoned or betrayed? How has that experience affected the way you view God?

- Read Deuteronomy 31:1–8 and Joshua 1:1–8. How many times do you see some version of "Be strong and courageous Do not be afraid. God will never leave you nor forsake you!"? Why do you think these phrases were repeated so often to the Israelites on the verge of entering their promised land? In what ways do you still need this reminder today?

- Read Isaiah 41:8–10. How do we see God as the compass and the constant companion in this passage? Why is it necessary for humanity to see God as both our compass and companion? In what ways is this a life-giving or crucial perspective for you?

- Read Matthew 28:16–20 and consider how it must have felt to be one of the disciples receiving this command from Jesus. What thoughts or emotions would you be thinking or feeling if that were you? How did the disciples respond to the Great Commission that Jesus gave them? How do you think things would have been different if Jesus had not promised to be with them "to the very end of the age"?

In a world in which very little remains constant, we can rest in the knowledge that our God will never leave us or forsake us.

• LESSON FOUR: READY OR NOT

In the middle of the pandemic of 2020, I sat down with two of my songwriting buddies and we chatted about how different things looked for us during those days. And though the loss of normal had made us feel disillusioned at times, we also acknowledged that it brought us to a place of expectancy. We confessed our fears and trepidation over canceled tours and schools still in limbo. Yet even though everything felt less settled and sturdy, we affirmed to each other how those circumstances had caused us to fall headlong into the waiting arms of our loving God. Yes, there was tremendous loss for each of us during those times. Yet, with eyes of faith we saw that every loss had a purpose. And every closed chapter marked the beginning of a new one, yet to be written. We spurred each other on to hope and to dream big for the next season. We encouraged each other to have mustard-seed-sized faith for whatever came next, whether we were ready or not.

You know, it's okay if you're not sure what your mission or calling should look like in your life. Or maybe you're tentative about letting go of your normal: your home, your self, your identity, your expectations, your comfort, and your security. That's to be expected. But this is where it all starts. It starts with accepting the invitation to climb up the tall tower, face our fear of heights, and take that first step off the platform. All God is asking of you right now is to take that first step. Often, that first step starts with these four simple words: *Lord Jesus, I'm willing.* Ready or not, may we say goodbye to normal with joy and expectation, knowing that God—our compass, our community, and our companion—has only the best in store for his children.

Reflect on these reminders of God's best and His help for your life:

> **"'For I know the plans I have for you,' declares the Lord, 'plans to prosper you and not to harm you, plans to give you hope and a future. Then you will call on me and come and pray to me, and I will listen to you. You will seek me and find me when you seek me with all your heart. I will be found by you,' declares the Lord, 'and will bring you back from captivity. I will gather you from all the nations and places where I have banished you,' declares the Lord, 'and will bring you back to the place from which I carried you into exile.'"**
>
> **Jeremiah 29:11–14 NIV**

> "For God so loved the world that he gave his one and only Son, that whoever believes in him shall not perish but have eternal life. For God did not send his Son into the world to condemn the world, but to save the world through him. Whoever believes in him is not condemned, but whoever does not believe stands condemned already because they have not believed in the name of God's one and only Son. This is the verdict: Light has come into the world, but people loved darkness instead of light because their deeds were evil. Everyone who does evil hates the light, and will not come into the light for fear that their deeds will be exposed. But whoever lives by the truth comes into the light, so that it may be seen plainly that what they have done has been done in the sight of God."
>
> **John 3:16–22 NIV**

> "But do not forget this one thing, dear friends: With the Lord a day is like a thousand years, and a thousand years are like a day. The Lord is not slow in keeping his promise, as some understand slowness. Instead he is patient with you, not wanting anyone to perish, but everyone to come to repentance."
>
> **2 Peter 3:8–9 NIV**

Name some of the ways you need God's help to take the first step into the unknown with him. What might it look like for you to prosper by letting go of normal and stepping into the unknown with him? What happens when you seek God with your whole heart into the unknown? In what ways does the love of God shine through the light in your life, even during uncertain times? How can you start to see God's slow and steady patience as his promise to you, rather than abandonment? Ready or not, what will it take for you to begin your first step into the unknown with God? Are you ready to pray *"Lord Jesus, I'm willing"*?

Because we know God to be true to his word, we do not need to fear even when stepping into uncharted territory.

• LESSON FIVE: EMBRACING THE UNKNOWN

I've shared a few real-life stories in both the video teaching and in my book *So Long, Normal* that have inspired and encouraged me on my own journey of saying so long to normal. Each of these people would say that their story isn't necessarily extraordinary in and of itself, but that God has done and is doing extraordinary things *through* their story. These stories are shared not to wow you, or to place any unrealistic expectations on you, but to encourage you to dream big about your own story, even when the journey ahead is unknown. I want to leave you with something concrete and applicable for your journey. So here's my invitation to you: *will you take a few moments to answer the same questions I asked the people I interviewed for the stories I've shared throughout this study?*

These questions will help make this experience personal to you. They are an opportunity to be honest with God and with yourself as you take a personal inventory of your life and consider the ways God may be working that perhaps you haven't recognized before.

My heartfelt prayer is that this exercise is one more step on your journey to confidently saying so long to normal and hello to God's glorious unknown.

Journal your answers to these questions. For the full version of these questions, read chapter 11 in So Long, Normal.

- Describe the normal you used to know. What was your childhood like, your religious background, your early view of God? If you are in a season of instability right now, can you identify a previous season that felt less shaky? Can you articulate what made that season feel more secure?

- What happened in your life to bring you to the place of saying so long to normal? Can you identify a traumatic event that caused a drifting or departure from the normal you used to know? How have you experienced change in your relationships, vocations, or surroundings, and what emotions accompanied this shift?

- What has been your steady? What has been your greatest source of comfort during life change: key people, organizations, practices, etc.? How has your faith sustained you, and how has your church community been a help during that season? How has God comforted you?

- What has been your gain? How has God used change in your life to teach you something about yourself *and* about himself? What blessings can you identify, and how have you been a blessing to others?

Pray for the strength and courage to fully embrace the unknown journey God is calling you to. Thank God for using broken people like me and you with broken stories to accomplish immeasurably more than we could ask or imagine. May God be pleased with our offering and may we be diligent to live out these truths by his grace. Amen.

It's not the greatness of our stories that makes them remarkable, but the greatness of God seen throughout our story.

RECOMMENDED READING

As you reflect on what God is teaching you through this last session, you may want to read chapter11 of *So Long, Normal* by Laura Story.

Here's a song I wrote, from me to you, as we say so long to normal and hello to the unknown, together:

Hello, Unknown

I've grown accustomed to the way things are
I'm way more comfortable when it's familiar
I want a life where I can guard my heart
Cause easy is easy

I like the solid ground beneath my feet
The kind of road that someone else paved before me
I need a plan that both my eyes can see
But you call me to mystery

I am letting go
Of everything I've known
Farewell, predictable
No more playing it safe
I'll free fall into faith
I'll say goodbye, control
Hello, Unknown

I'm prone to find a way to skip the hard
The very trials you would use to refine me
There's beauty you create through every scar
If only I'm willing
Lord Jesus, I'm willing

What if I follow where you lead,
What if the narrow road is steep,
You know the plans you have for me.
What if it's through the valley deep,
What if it's only you and me,
I still have everything I need.
Jesus, you are everything I need.

Epilogue

We made it!

We made it to the mountaintop of the unknown after saying so long to normal, loosening our grip and letting go of whatever has been keeping us steady up until this point, saying yes to our new life in Christ, and stepping out into the unknown with God. What a journey this has been.

Some of you may still be wrestling with doubt, insecurity, or unbelief—just like the father of a young boy in need of healing who questioned if Jesus could really heal his son, and then cried out, "I believe. Help my unbelief" (Mark 9:23–25). If that's you, it's okay. It's okay to be in that place, as long as you don't stay there. You *can* step out in faith and say yes to following God into the unknown even if you're not so sure you're ready to be on the journey. God is big enough to handle all of our fear, doubt, anxiety, bad past experiences, and unbelief. He loves us too much to leave us right where we are.

Because I believe all good concerts, church services, Bible studies, and retreats end with a benediction and blessing, here is mine for you:

I pray you've sensed my heart as I've shared biblical principles and real-life stories that have helped me on my own journey in saying so long to normal.

I pray I've encouraged you to step out in boldness, step away from unhealthy or overly cautious patterns of life, and truly say goodbye to anything upon which you lean as a substitute for true faith.

I pray that we would never again settle for normal when God desires for us the extraordinary.

And I pray that even in times of grieving for the loss of normal, you will grieve with hope, knowing that God's plan for you is good and that he never leaves you to grieve alone.

May you trust the love of God to lead you into the great unknown knowing that he works all things together for our good and his greater glory.

Grace and peace to you,

Laura

> **"Now to him who is able to do immeasurably more than all we ask or imagine, according to his power that is at work within us, to him be glory in the church and in Christ Jesus throughout all generations, for ever and ever! Amen."**
>
> **Ephesians 3:20–21 NIV**

Leader's Guide

Thank you for your willingness to lead your group through this study! What you have chosen to do is valuable and will make a great difference in the lives of others. The rewards of being a leader are different from those of participating, and we hope that as you lead you will find your own walk with Jesus deepened by this experience.

So Long, Normal is a five-session study built around video content and small-group interaction. As the group leader, simply think of yourself as the host of a dinner party. Your job is to take care of your participants by managing all the behind-the-scenes details so that when everyone arrives, they can just enjoy time together.

As the group leader, your role is not to answer all the questions or reteach the content—the video, book, and study guide will do most of that work. Your job is to guide the experience and cultivate your small group into a kind of learning community. This will make it a place for members to process, question, and reflect—not receive more instruction.

Before your first meeting, make sure everyone in the group gets a copy of the study guide. This will keep everyone on the same page and help the process run more smoothly. If some group members are unable to purchase the guide, arrange it so that people can share the resource with other group members. Giving everyone access to all the material will position this study to be as rewarding an experience as possible. Everyone should feel free to write in his or her study guide and bring it to the group every week.

SETTING UP THE GROUP

You will need to determine with your group how long you want to meet each week so you can plan your time accordingly. Generally, most groups like to meet for either ninety minutes or two hours, so you could use one of the following schedules:

Section	90 Minutes	120 Minutes
Introduction (members arrive and get settled)	10 minutes	15 minutes
Talk about it (discuss one or more of the opening questions for the session)	10 minutes	15 minutes
Watch (watch the teaching material together and take notes)	25 minutes	25 minutes
Discuss (discuss the Bible study questions you selected ahead of time)	35 minutes	50 minutes
Respond / Pray (read the memory verse and pray together as a group, then dismiss)	10 minutes	15 minutes

As the group leader, you'll want to create an environment that encourages sharing and learning. A church sanctuary or formal classroom may not be as ideal as a living room, because those locations can feel formal and less intimate. No matter what setting you choose, provide enough comfortable seating for everyone, and, if possible, arrange the seats in a semicircle so everyone can see the video easily. This will make the transition between the video and group conversation more efficient and natural.

Also, try to get to the meeting site early so you can greet participants as they arrive. Simple refreshments create a welcoming atmosphere and can be a wonderful addition to a group study evening. Try to take food and pet allergies into account to make your guests as comfortable as possible. You may also want to consider offering childcare to couples with children who want to attend. Finally, be sure your media technology is working properly. Managing these details upfront will make the rest of your group experience flow smoothly and provide a welcoming space in which to engage the content of *So Long, Normal*.

STARTING THE GROUP TIME

Once everyone has arrived, it's time to begin the group. Here are some simple tips to make your group time healthy, enjoyable, and effective.

First, begin the meeting with a short prayer and remind the group members to put their phones on silent. This is a way to make sure you can all be present with one another and with God. Next, give each person a few minutes to respond to the questions in the "Talk About It" section. This won't require as much time in session one, but beginning in session two, people will need more time to share their insights from their personal studies. Usually, you won't answer the discussion questions yourself, but you should go first with the "Talk About It" questions, answering briefly and with a reasonable amount of transparency.

At the end of session one, invite the group members to complete the between-sessions personal studies for that week. Explain that you will be providing some time before the video teaching next week for anyone to share insights. Let them know sharing is optional, and it's no problem if they can't get to some of the between-sessions activities some weeks. It will still be beneficial for them to hear from the other participants and learn about what they discovered.

LEADING THE DISCUSSION TIME

Now that the group is engaged, it's time to watch the video and respond with some directed small-group discussion. Encourage all the group members to participate in the discussion, but make sure they know they don't have to do so. As the discussion progresses, you may want to follow up with comments such as, "Tell me more about that," or, "Why did you answer that way?" This will allow the group participants to deepen their reflections and invite meaningful sharing in a non-threatening way.

Note that you have been given multiple questions to use in each session, and you do not have to use them all or even follow them in order. Feel free to pick and choose questions based on either the needs of your group or how the conversation is flowing. Also, don't be afraid of silence. Offering a question and allowing up to thirty seconds of silence is okay. It allows people space to think about how they want to respond and also gives them time to do so.

As the group leader, you are the boundary keeper for your group. Do not let anyone (yourself included) dominate the group time. Keep an eye out for group members who might be tempted to "attack" folks they disagree with or try to "fix" those having struggles. These kinds of behaviors can derail a group's momentum, so they need to be steered in a different direction. Model active listening and encourage everyone in your group to do the same. This will make your group time a safe space and create a positive community.

The group discussion leads to a closing time of individual reflection and prayer. Encourage the participants to take a few moments to review what they've learned during the session and write down their thoughts after the Group Discussion. This will help them cement the big ideas in their minds as you close the session. Conclude by having the participants break into smaller groups of two to three people to pray for one another.

Thank you again for taking the time to lead your group. You are making a difference in the lives of others and having an impact on the kingdom of God!

COMPANION BOOK TO ENRICH YOUR STUDY EXPERIENCE

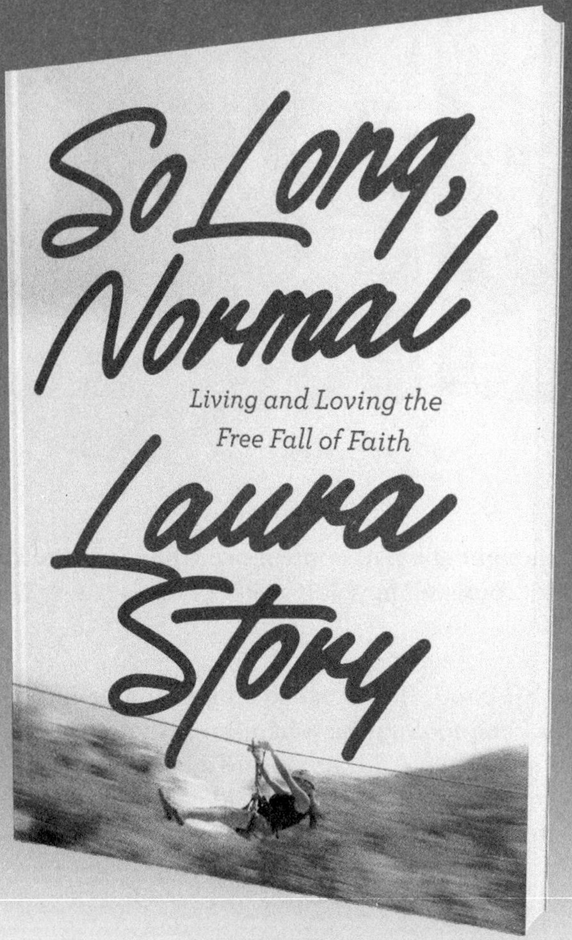

ISBN 9780785248521

Available wherever books are sold.

W Publishing Group